THE WARRIOR'S HEART

Becoming a Man of Compassion and Courage

Eric Greitens, Navy SEAL

Houghton Mifflin Harcourt
Boston   New York

To my teachers at McKelvey Elementary, Parkway East
Junior High, and Parkway North High School:
This book is dedicated to your patience,
your wisdom, and your encouragement.

Copyright © 2012 by Eric Greitens

All rights reserved. Originally published in hardcover in the United States by Houghton
Mifflin, an imprint of Houghton Mifflin Harcourt Publishing Company, 2012.

For information about permission to reproduce selections from this book, write to
Permissions, Houghton Mifflin Harcourt Publishing Company, 215 Park Avenue South,
New York, New York 10003.

www.hmhco.com

The text of this book is set in Bembo.

Edited by Emma D. Dryden
Book design by Carol Chu

Library of Congress Cataloging-in-Publication Data is on file.

ISBN: 978-0-547-86852-3 hardcover
ISBN: 978-0-544-10481-5 paperback

Manufactured in the U.S.A.
DOC 10 9 8 7 6 5 4 3 2

4500525945

Books by Eric Greitens

Strength and Compassion: Photographs and Essays

*The Heart and the Fist: The Education of a Humanitarian,
the Making of a Navy SEAL*

*The Warrior's Heart: Becoming a Man of Compassion
and Courage*

YOU

You stand in freezing water up to your chest. Every muscle in your body throbs with pain. You are exhausted beyond anything you could ever imagine, and all around you the night air carries the curses and groans of others who are gutting it out like you, who are trying to survive the night.

Most won't.

You know the statistics: Maybe one in ten will make it through this week, will survive hours—days—of the punishment required to become a Navy SEAL.

The water is dark around you, but you can make out lights on the beach. You remember your instructors' words as the sun drifted toward the horizon, their voices booming over the bullhorns:

"Say good night to the sun, gentlemen, say good night to the sun."

"Tonight is going to be a very, very long night, gentlemen."

"Tonight is going to be a very, very long night."

You imagine another hundred hours of this. You see yourself plunging over and over into the icy water, pulling yourself out again. You imagine endless repetitions of sit-ups, flutter kicks, pushups. Surf torture, they call it, when they leave you in freezing water. Not just for a few minutes but for five more days. Five days of struggle and uncertainty. Five days of physical and emotional torment made to separate the iron-willed from the merely strong.

In the distance, a bell sounds three times. And then another three times. As you hear the bell, you know that another student has chosen to quit.

A voice rises and falls, taunting you, inviting you to do the same. "Quit now, and you can avoid the rush later. It just gets colder. It just gets harder."

One by one, sometimes in clusters, other students surrender. All around you, they slog up out of the water, bodies shivering, clothes soaked. They climb up out of the ocean, walk up the sand hill. And they ring the bell.

For them, it is the end.

The others in your crew struggle along with you, and it's their companionship and their strength that buoys you. You are there for one another. You are a team, and you do not want to quit on your team.

But you are bone-tired and shivering. You're afraid you'll never make it through this night, let alone an entire week.

On shore stands a brightly lit tent. Others are gathered inside, their palms cupping mugs of warm coffee. They are wrapped in blankets, eating hamburgers. They are safe.

You could be one of them.

All you have to do is rise out of the icy water and walk toward the tent. It's easy. Students have been doing it all *night. Just get up. Get out. Walk toward that bell and quit.*

Then you could be warm and dry like the others. Then your stomach could be full, and you could feel your fingers and toes again.

All you have to do is get up, get out. Ring the bell.

What do you do?

ADVENTURE AWAITS

Goose bumps rose as my flashlight brightened the words in front of me:

Beware and Warning! This book is different from other books. You and YOU ALONE are in charge of what happens in this story. . . . You are a deep sea explorer searching for the famed lost city of Atlantis. This is your most challenging and dangerous mission. Fear and excitement are now your companions.[1]

At two in the morning, I was supposed to be asleep, not hidden beneath my blanket, reading until my eyes grew sore and I passed out with my face mashed against a book cover.

But as a kid growing up in Missouri, I couldn't get enough of these stories, the ones that put you right into the adventure, that pulled you into a vivid world and then asked *you* to decide which path to take. Should you investigate the mysterious underwater grotto, or stay in your submarine to analyze the odd bubbles rising from the canyon floor? Should you follow the call of the Himalayan Yeti, or return to the safety of base camp?

Each choice scared and thrilled me. I gobbled the books whole, going back to redo any bad decisions that led to my untimely demise.

Like many American kids, I grew up learning about a world populated by heroes. I read about Pericles, who built democracy in ancient Greece. I read about King Arthur and the medieval Knights of the Round Table, who fought sorcerers and giants and protected the weak. And I read about great American heroes: George Washington, who crossed a frozen Delaware River and led America through revolution to victory; Abraham Lincoln, whose words at Gettysburg laid the Civil War dead to rest and called a nation to its duty; Martin Luther King Jr., who announced to the world, "I have a dream," and inspired Americans to struggle for justice and dignity.

I loved history, and I liked to imagine myself as part of it. But this rich view of the world also left me wondering where I fit in. My big fear was that God and my parents had made a terrible mistake and that I'd been born in the wrong era, that the time for adventures had passed. I sat in the St. Louis public library and read stories of people discovering ancient cities and settling wild frontiers. I read about warriors, explorers, and activists, and then I'd stare out the window at a world that seemed very small and very safe.

I was worried that all the corners of the earth had been explored, all the great battles fought. The famous people on TV were athletes and actresses and singers. What did they stand for? I wondered: *Had the time for heroes passed?*

My other fear was that I'd miss my chance at a meaningful life. My mom was an early childhood special education teacher, and my dad was an accountant. They'd told me—perhaps since kindergarten—that I should work hard so I could go to a place called college. College, they promised, was "the ticket."

I imagined the ticket as something golden and shiny, like a ticket for a train that would hurtle me to a place filled with adventures. As I understood it, they gave out tickets after high school, but if you wanted one, you had to have good grades.

So in third grade, when I came home with a report card that read: "Eric Greitens, Handwriting: B−," I naturally asked my mom, "Will they still let me go to college?"

She laughed and hugged me.

My parents wanted me to treat others with kindness. They wanted me to be respectful. They wanted me to try hard and to be a team player. But while they cared about these "character" things, they didn't seem so concerned with whether or not I got great grades. Especially at eight years old.

When my third grade science fair experiment—involving tulips, soda, and my dad's beer—ended in catastrophe, I asked again, "Will they still let me go to college?"

When at ten years old, I lit a pile of leaves on fire to keep myself warm while waiting for the school bus and managed to accidentally set a whole sewer full of dry leaves on fire, I asked: "Will they still let me go to college?"

It was in college, everyone told me over and over, that I could pursue big dreams. College was the first step into the "real world," where every great purpose could be pursued. In college, my adventures would really begin.

GETTING IT RIGHT

My parents weren't rich, which meant I'd have to find a way to pay for college myself. As a kid, I didn't think about scholarships or loans; I thought about earning money. My dad had set up a savings account for me at the local credit union, and he'd show me the bank statement every month so I could see the bits of interest adding to my account.

At any rate, I knew I'd have to start earning as much money as I could, as soon as I could, in order to get where I wanted to go.

But how? At ten, I had limited options. I checked out some books from the library on how to run a small business, but I didn't find much inspiration there. For a while I tried clipping coupons out of the newspaper and then selling them to adults for just a little less than the face value. But for all the clipping and walking around the neighborhood I did, I only made a few dimes each week.

How else did kids make money? I racked my brain. Lemonade stand? I pictured myself sitting behind a cardboard box, waiting for customers to appear. It seemed too boring. And how many thirsty people could I count on to walk by each day?

No. I needed something more active, a job where I could seek out customers and persuade them to hire me. I settled on mowing lawns and raking leaves. At the top of a notebook where I kept track of my jobs, I wrote: GREITENS LAWN CARE.

Eventually, it would grow to be a booming enterprise, complete with subcontractors (my younger brothers). My company handled not just raking leaves but edging lawns, weeding, trimming hedges, painting, and—best of all—shoveling snow in the winter. I cut a deal with my neighbor. He said that if I cleared his driveway for free every time it snowed, I could use his snowblower on other neighbors' driveways. So my brothers and I would walk through the neighborhood pushing the snowblower in front of us, shovels on our shoulders, asking neighbors if they wanted us to clear their driveways.

One of my first customers was Roger Richardson, husband of my kindergarten teacher, Anne Richardson. Roger taught history at the high school and coached football. In addition to being one of my first clients, he taught me a lot of valuable skills, such as how to tie certain knots, how to be safe working with electricity, how to lay bricks and mortar, and the right way to paint.

He also taught me a valuable lesson about doing a job right.

Once, one of my brothers and I had spent a tough afternoon working on Roger's yard, mowing grass and trimming trees. We were supposed to collect all the branches and sticks, tie them into bundles, and put them out for trash collection. It was a hot day, and, exhausted, we forgot that we'd left a bunch of sticks on Roger's front porch.

To his credit, when Roger called my house, he asked to

speak to me instead of telling my mom what we'd done—or hadn't done.

"Eric," he said. "You need to come back and finish the job."

The walk to Roger's house seemed like the longest of my life. I knew I hadn't done a good job, and as reluctant as I was to go face the music, I was also determined to show him I could get it done right. Not only did I tie up each and every stick in a neat bundle for the trash collectors, I made sure to straighten all the gardening tools in the shed, and I swept his porch and driveway.

I worked for Roger for the next eight years, until I left for college. Every summer I mowed his lawn, and every winter I shoveled his driveway.

Working for him and others gave me a concrete understanding of money and how it worked. For years, if I was going to buy something, I'd translate the purchase into the number of lawns I'd mowed to earn it.

A movie and ice cream with a date in high school?

That equaled two and a half lawns.

College?

That was going to require an awful lot of raking and snow blowing.

I like to think that working for Roger prepped me for military training. He taught me that it wasn't enough to have a job. To make a job meaningful, you had to pay attention to the details and take pride in your work. He taught me the importance of getting it right. Since then, I've used those lessons a thousand times.

A LESSON IN RESPECT

Even before college, other lessons came my way. One of the most important was that to be great or really do good in the world, I needed to understand the world beyond myself.

When I was sixteen years old, Bruce Carl—the director of Youth Leadership St. Louis—took me and a few other students to spend the night in a homeless shelter downtown.

Bruce was a former basketball player with a lithe build, a shock of dark hair, and bright eyes. He bounded through life with the happy energy of a man who had good news to share. As director of the city's youth leadership program, he encouraged us to question authority and to serve. He was one of the first men to teach me that you could be a hero without slaying a dragon or leading a victory charge. You could make a difference in a quiet way and still have a profound impact on others.

Bruce took our group to the shelter because he wanted to impress upon us that it was important to understand how our neighbors lived.

In my mind, I was about to embark on a small adventure. I was sixteen, away from my parents on a mission into the unknown. I was curious to know what was out there. Bruce knew this. He also realized that whether we wanted to or not, we were there to learn what life was like for people who struggled every day.

Before we entered the building, he looked at us and said, "I want you to listen. Learn."

And so on a winter night in a downtown church, I sipped chicken soup from a Styrofoam cup, crackers floating, softening, and breaking apart as I talked with homeless men. When we bedded down for the night, it was in a room that smelled of urine and body odor, on threadbare green mats laid on top of old cots.

I thought about meals with my family, about holiday dinners with platter after platter of food. I thought about being warm in my own bed, in my own room, secure in the knowledge that someone nearby cared about me. I thought about the used car I'd just purchased with the money I'd earned from mowing lawns, and what a luxury that would be to some of these people. And I thought—with embarrassment—that I had seen men like these before, pushing carts along downtown streets, gathering outside churches and community organizations that served hot meals. But I hadn't really *seen* them, not like I was doing here, as I sat with them and listened. And learned.

When one of the men mentioned his job, my face betrayed my surprise, and he said, "You thought none of us had a job?"

My face grew warm. "Yes, I did think that," I said. "I'm sorry."

"Don't apologize, young man. How about you just work my shift tomorrow?" He burst out laughing, and the rest of the night he kept telling everyone, "Young man here gonna work my shift tomorrow. He gonna work my shift."

Later I stood with two men at a window looking out on the freezing St. Louis night. As the shelter doors were locked, I saw a man walking hunched over on the other side of the street. He seemed thin and underdressed as he leaned into the icy wind.

"Tonight's a bad night to be out," said one of the men.

Later that night Bruce sat down next to me, a somber expression on his face. "This is terrible," he said, surprising me. I'd never really seen him down before.

"What's wrong?" I asked.

He lowered his voice and leaned in so only I could hear. "They're giving food and shelter, but they don't have any job training or substance-abuse programs. They keep running things this way, and these people will stay homeless forever."

Just as Bruce had challenged us by bringing us to the shelter, he wanted to see the men in the shelter challenged as well. Just as he respected us, he respected the homeless men, and he believed that if you respected someone, you had to ask something of them.

These men, he believed, should be involved in their own recovery.

He thought it criminal that people could grow up oblivious and unresponsive to the suffering of others. "These are your *neighbors,*" he would say. But he was pragmatic enough to know that having a loving, wide-open heart was only a start. If you wanted to make a change, you had to arm yourself with a plan and with the knowledge and resources to put that plan into action.

All of which pointed me back to the golden ticket to my intended destination: college. There, I thought, I'd learn how to really make a difference. There I'd learn the skills that would help me channel the compassion of people like Bruce to bring about a better world.

THE WORLD OPENS

So I went to college. But for the first few weeks, I felt I'd been lied to.

I'd chosen Duke University. Its unofficial motto, "Work hard, play hard," appealed to me. Duke also offered me a scholarship that covered my tuition for four years and included a summer term at Oxford University in England between my junior and senior years. I was extraordinarily grateful for the opportunities that Duke offered me.

I decided to study public policy because it concerned—I believed—the great affairs of the world. It was the study of all we had in common and how we could improve the world together. I'd been lucky in elementary, junior high, and high school because so many of my teachers had taught us about other countries and cultures. They'd challenged us to debate social and political questions and to analyze America's role in the world and our way of life.

Yet in my first college class, Introduction to Public Policy Studies, the professor droned, "First, we calculate the values of the proposed outcomes." He scratched a graph on the chalkboard. "Then we assess the probability of achieving those outcomes." He scratched again. "And then we multiply." He scratched a final time. "Now we know what decision to make."

This was public policy? Great decisions about the fate of the world made through multiplication? When were we going to talk about how to live well, how to lead, what to fight for? How was I going to learn what I needed to know to help men like those I'd met in the shelter?

I thought that in college we would dive into the deep pools of the world's wisdom. Instead I was being taught how to plot decision trees.

I struggled. I considered a new major. I talked with everyone who would meet with me. Pretty soon I recognized that my journey wasn't going to be handed to me. I remembered the books I'd loved as a kid and realized: *I have to choose my own adventure.*

So I looked for opportunities, and one day I saw my chance. In the student newspaper, I discovered a notice about grants that were available to conduct independent-study projects overseas during the summer. They'd give preference to applicants like me who had never been abroad before.

I tucked the newspaper under my arm and walked to class. I felt eager, exhilarated. Suddenly, the expansive grounds and Gothic architecture of Duke looked more majestic to me, richer, the way things often look when you're about to leave them.

The grant offered a chance to see the world. Where should I go?

YOU: NAMING NAMES

You sit behind a long metal table at a police station in Beijing. The room is warm and empty except for a filing cabinet, the table, and a couple of chairs. A lone light bulb dangles from a string over your head, casting dull shadows against the somber gray walls.

Two police officers—one in uniform, one in plain clothes—sit with you, urging you to take a cigarette from the pack they extend politely. They came to your dormitory room to get you, driving you to the station with your friend, whom you hear crying in another room. You are more worried about her than you are about yourself, but you have no idea why you've been brought here, what will happen, or who you can call for help.

The police question you about your job, about the English class you've been teaching to a small group of Chinese workers. The questions are simple at first, easy enough to answer. You tell them that you teach English and some grammar. That your friends and colleagues connected you with the job.

The energy of the room focuses, turns sharper somehow.

The uniformed officer asks, "Who in the class asks questions about American government?"

They look at you expectantly. The sound of your friend's crying grows louder. You see how to help yourself. All you have to do is give them the names of a few students, tell them what they want to know. Then you can probably leave.

"Who in the class asks questions about freedom of speech?" asks the other officer. His eyes drill into you.

Just a few names, that's all. Then you can get out of this oppressive room. Then you can go back to your dormitory, enjoy your last few days in China, and head back to the safety of home.

What do you do?

THE OTHER SIDE OF THE WORLD

Can you imagine caring so deeply about an ideal that you'd plant yourself in the path of an oncoming tank to defend your beliefs? Can you see yourself standing firm with thousands of other unarmed students while soldiers bear down with riot gear and guns? And can you imagine that what you're fighting for, the thing that someone brutally opposes, is your right to make your own choices, to believe what you want to believe, read what you want to read, say what you feel moved to say?

At fifteen years old, I'd watched the massacre of Chinese students in Beijing on television. I was just a little younger than those I saw in photos, and yet the whole event felt remote from my safe life in suburban St. Louis. I took a lot for granted back then: the right I'd someday have to vote, to travel to any part of the world, to voice my disapproval of things that seemed unjust, to make decisions for myself.

And now, at age eighteen and faced with a big life-changing decision—where to go, among all the places that fired my imagination—I chose China.

Why? Well, I'd like to say the decision took a lot of deep thought and careful weighing of options, but really it came about because my uncle was in the broom business and had once made a trip to China to visit a broom factory. My uncle offered to help me, so I put together a grant application to study in China.

When the grant came through, I couldn't believe I'd be traveling halfway around the world. I'd barely been out of the Midwest before. When I left for the airport, I knew zero about Chinese culture. I didn't speak a word of Mandarin. And I knew almost nothing about Chinese history.

I did, however, own a new hat. Inspired by Indiana Jones, I went to the mall and bought one. Only, I couldn't find a sharp-looking fedora like Indy's. Instead, as I walked through the airport with a brand-new pack on my back, I sported an Australian outback hat on my head. Close enough.

I was ready for adventure.

Getting there meant flying from St. Louis to Dallas to San Francisco to Beijing. I felt like I'd crossed the world before I even left the country. On the final leg of the trip, I sat next to an elderly Chinese woman. She asked me my family name, and I told her, "It's Greitens, pronounced like 'brightens' with a 'G.'"

"In China, you'll be better off as 'Mr. Eric,'" she said. Then she taught me a few key phrases. By the time we landed, I was able to say, "I am hungry. Feed me."

I woke the next morning jet-lagged and thirsty. Everyone in America had warned me over and over again that even *touching* the water in China would lead to dysentery, diarrhea, diphtheria, and a host of other savage-sounding illnesses. I had purchased a contraption to boil water, but after five minutes of unsuccessfully trying to boil a cup of water in the hotel bathroom, I opened the faucet, filled a glass of water, and drank.

Before leaving for my trip, I had put my finger on a globe at the position of St. Louis, Missouri, and another finger on Beijing. Those inches took me more than a day's travel to accomplish. But now I stood on the other side of the world. A wide smile broke across my face.

I went to the window and opened the curtains on a bright, beautiful Beijing day. I looked down on a street teeming with commuters pedaling bicycles. I was really here. I was abroad. I was traveling. The life I'd imagined—the one filled with remarkable moments and adventures—lay right before me.

My plan was to go to Changchun, a city in the northeast of the country that I'd heard referred to as "China's Detroit" because of its manufacturing. I would study China's emerging business sector—satisfying the academic requirements of the trip—and I would get to know the country.

China had just begun to open to Western tourists, and Changchun was not a popular destination. With the exception of a few Germans at a Volkswagen plant, I met no other foreigners in the city.

Changchun was sprawling, with wide avenues and thousands of pedestrians. Its population was more than ten times that of St. Louis, and my trips to the factories were interesting, but I felt isolated there. My inability to speak Chinese kept me from interacting meaningfully with anyone. So when the receptionist at my hotel invited me to join her kung fu class, I happily accepted. I was ready for my next challenge.

KUNG FU

We arrived at a school gymnasium at four thirty the next morning. The *shifu*—meaning "teacher-father" in Chinese—was about five feet five inches of packed muscle beneath a gray crew cut. I guessed he was about sixty years old. He wore a light blue cotton shirt fastened with embroidered ties instead of buttons, cuffs folded back against the sleeves.

He prowled gracefully among the rows of students engaged in their *taolu*—a fight dance of choreographed punches, kicks, and blocks. I loved sports, and I couldn't wait to get started.

The *shifu* came up to me, his movements fluid and unassuming. I stood up straight and smiled. I wanted to show him I'd be a great student.

The *shifu* called the other students over, and they gathered around us. I held my breath, wondering what was about to happen. He regarded me for a moment and placed a fist against my chest, barely touching me. With a hoarse shout, he opened his fist and knocked me backwards into the wall.

I leaned there, dazed, while the other students nodded dutifully. It felt like he'd knocked the wind out of me *and* my entire family.

The *shifu* helped me to stand upright. I'd almost gotten to the "you" in "thank you" when he knocked me backwards again.

My friend the hotel receptionist explained, "*Shifu* punch you to show how to destroy enemy."

The *shifu* smiled at me, nodded. I smiled back. I had no idea what had just happened, but it seemed to me that I'd just been accepted as a student.

The assistant *shifu* was a police officer in his midthirties. Each day he wore what looked to me like a pair of loose black pajamas. If I'd met him on the street, I would have thought: *short, tubby guy.* He seemed unremarkable, but when he stood on one leg to demonstrate a strike or when he kicked at a target six and a half feet off the ground, he moved with incredible power.

He spent a lot of time with me, patiently demonstrating moves, returning to me time after time during practice.

One day he spoke earnestly to me, and my friend translated: "The assistant *shifu* says you must learn kung fu well. If you go back to America and are bad, he will be shamed."

I certainly didn't want to shame him — or myself. I tried hard in class, but always came away feeling clumsy and stiff. Once, when I was practicing a set of strikes, the assistant *shifu* came up behind me, grabbed my chin with his right hand, and put his left hand on the base of my neck. His hands twisted, and I heard every vertebra in my neck pop like a thunderclap of cracked knuckles. I expected to fall to the ground like a rag doll with a broken spine, but instead I just felt . . . better. A little more loose and agile.

I kept at it for weeks. Finally, graduation day arrived, and though I'd basically just stumbled into the class, it felt important somehow that I graduate.

In order to do so, I had to pass a series of tests. In the first test, a student stood with his legs spread as if riding an invisible horse, hands together in front of his chest as if in prayer, eyes focused straight ahead. He was grounding himself, centering his *chi*—or inner power.

The assistant *shifu* set a coiled rag on top of the student's head. Then he set one red brick on the rag. Atop that, he set another brick and then another. It looked to me like a balancing exercise to test how still the student could remain as he was loaded down with bricks. Four bricks were stacked on the student's head. I thought, *I can do that.*

They placed a folding chair next to the student, and the *shifu* stood on its seat. He gave a command, and the assistant *shifu* ran to the corner of the room and returned with a sledgehammer.

When I saw the sledgehammer, I gulped and said a small prayer. I prayed in English and thought I'd been quiet, but somehow everyone in the room—who'd apparently understood the test from the beginning—seemed to get that until that moment I'd had no idea what was happening. They all smiled.

I tried not to gasp as the *shifu* swung the sledgehammer in a wide arc and brought it down on the top brick. The bricks cracked clean down the middle, straight to the final brick, and the broken halves fell on either side of the student. Now standing in a pile of debris, the student turned and bowed dutifully to the *shifu,* apparently thanking him for the experience. The student walked back to his classmates with a smile.

I was next in line.

Feeling a rush of fear, I held up my hands and protested in English: "No, I'm sorry, that's . . ." I wanted to say, "That's a little advanced for me" or "That's not going to turn out well for my head," but I could only stammer.

Okay, they said. I could take the tests in any order.

The assistant *shifu* drew a sword. I watched again as one of the students centered his *chi* and grounded himself. The *shifu* placed the pointy edge of the sword against the student's throat and pushed.

I held my breath, sure the sword would go straight through the man's neck. But as the *shifu* pulled the sword away, I saw that he'd left only a small red scratch. I exhaled.

When the assistant *shifu* approached me, I stepped back, thinking to skip this test too. But he spoke forcefully to my friend.

She turned to me and translated: "The *shifu* says it would be very bad for Chinese kung fu if you die. The test is important for their honor and for yours. He says that you can pass if you try."

I knew my family would take little consolation in the knowledge that I had given my life "in honor of Chinese kung fu," but I stepped forward. I set my hands in prayer in front of my chest, and as the *shifu* put the point of the sword against my neck, I focused all of my energy on my throat. He pushed. I felt the steel point of the blade against my neck, and then suddenly I was bowing. I had passed the test.

I left class that day with an appreciation of kung fu. I also left with a pair of steel railroad-spike nunchucks and a sword. I was nineteen years old and never thought I would need these or any other weapons. For me, the world's violence happened offstage. I wanted to make a contribution somehow, somewhere — but I didn't think that my fight would be with weapons.

LANGUAGE BARRIER

I wanted to make more of my time in China, so later in the summer I went back to Beijing. There, Han Lin—a friend of a friend of my uncle's—helped me to get a job at her company, teaching English in the afternoons. The workers lived in dormitories, and between my stay there and teaching in the classroom, I thought it would be a great way to connect with other people my age.

I expected only a few students for my first class, so when three or four people walked in, I said hello and tried to make small talk. A few more students arrived, followed by several more. Soon I had a small classroom packed with fifteen students eager to learn English. As they greeted me, I heard a wide range of abilities. Some of the students were almost fluent; others struggled with "How are you?"

Standing in front of the class, I felt keenly aware of the attention focused on me. I had no idea how to teach English, let alone how to teach students at so many levels of ability all at once. I decided to open the class for discussion. A few people would get something out of the dialogue, I hoped, and the others might start to follow along eventually.

I introduced myself, then said, "I'd like to learn together. What do you want to talk about?"

A hand shot up. "Mr. Erica, what is freedom of speech in America?"

It seemed an odd first question, but every pair of eyes fixed on me, waiting for an answer. I wondered how to explain what to me felt like a very basic concept, a fact of life I'd never really questioned.

"Well, in America we have one document that forms the basis for our government. That document is the Constitution, and it includes a Bill of Rights that gives rights to every citizen. One of those is the right to say almost anything you like." I wanted to explain more, but it was clear I'd already lost some of the class.

The others looked at me raptly, and another hand shot up. "Mr. Erica, what is freedom of assembly mean for you?"

A student to my right glanced nervously at the door, then rose from his chair and shut it. I assumed he was concerned that our voices might disturb others in the building, and I continued on, answering as best I could.

The third question was also about the Bill of Rights.

Many of the students in the class were in their early to midtwenties, and I soon found out that they had been student activists at Tiananmen Square in 1989. I was the first Westerner most of them had spoken to since the protests. The room came alive with dozens of eager hands, and for over an hour I did my best to explain what Americans thought about what had happened at Tiananmen.

Luckily, they were not looking to me as an authority on democracy or as the definitive guide on American public opinion. Most just wanted to know what Americans thought about what they had lived through.

After class a group of us rode bicycles to dinner. We continued our discussion over dumplings and vegetables.

We spoke in hushed voices. The student who had closed the classroom door explained, "Mr. Erica, the government does not like us to talk about June 4 [the date of the worst violence in Beijing]."

One girl described the days she had spent with her friends at the demonstrations. In halting English, she told me that she felt they'd change history. She had missed the violence in the early morning of June 4, but a friend of hers had helped carry another bleeding friend out of the square and to an apartment for medical care.

I remembered TV footage of tanks, trucks full of soldiers, and crowds of students. Chaos and confusion reigned as reporters announced that shots were being fired at unarmed protesters. I remembered images of the protester who stood in the path of rolling tanks. As one of the tanks pivoted to drive around him, the man moved and blocked the tank's path again. As the tank tried to maneuver past him once more, he stood his ground.

I had watched them on TV, and now I saw that those courageous activists were very real people. Some of them liked soy sauce on their dumplings; others drank more than they ate. Some of them were unshaven, some of them joked constantly, and some had big dreams of going to America.

History came alive for me in that moment. It was made by regular people. Courageous, determined, thoughtful people—students my age—who'd withstood violence and who, even now, took risks just by discussing what people the world over had witnessed.

I had an amazing time riding my bicycle to and from work, teaching in the afternoons, going out for dinner with my new friends, and talking for hours into the night. Many had dreams of traveling to the United States, and they peppered me with questions:

"How much does an apartment cost in Los Angeles?"

"Do they have rock 'n' roll clubs in Boston or only in Memphis?"

"How hard is it to get a job in America?"

"How hard is it to get a scholarship?"

Their excitement made me look at my life and at my country differently. It wasn't that I thought America was perfect, but their enthusiasm made me see that we still stood as a beacon of freedom to people in other countries. We still offered ideals to which others aspired.

One night in the dormitory, when only two other people were in the room, one of my new friends placed a small canister of film in my hand.

He looked anxiously at the closed door and whispered, "These are photos I took of June 4 protests, but I cannot develop them. Please take them home and develop them. Know what really happened here."

I felt a rush of adrenaline, as if I'd joined an underground resistance movement. I took the film canister and shook his hand.

Later, when I developed the film, I found image after image of students holding protest signs. The pictures weren't particularly violent or incendiary, but they had a quiet power to them. Seeing them awakened in me a desire to capture the world in the same way. My lifelong love of photography was born.

INTERROGATION

One Friday night, a group of us gathered in the workers' dormitory to play darts. A knock came at the door, and two police officers stepped into the room. They spoke to my friends, who then turned to me, faces pale, and said, "Mr. Erica, the policeman wants you go to police station."

I looked anxiously from my friends to the police officers. "Why?"

"To make paperwork."

I looked at my watch: nine o'clock. It seemed like a bad idea to go off with these officers at night, "to make paperwork."

"Please explain that I would be pleased to come to the police station on Saturday morning or on Monday morning," I said. "But I cannot go with them at nine o'clock on a Friday night."

This was translated to the police officers. The officers spoke again to my friends, and my friends turned back to me.

"Mr. Erica, you are going to the police station—now."

Han Lin and I were driven to the police station in the back

seat of a police car, accompanied by another man from the dormitory.

"They can't do anything to us," he whispered, though his eyes darted nervously toward the men in the front seat. "China is different now."

I wasn't sure about that, but I certainly hoped it was true.

At the police station, they directed us to a waiting area, where we sat on green couches and whispered to one another. I still had no idea what they wanted from me, what "paperwork" needed my urgent attention.

At about ten o'clock, they called us down a hallway. I followed Han Lin, but they directed her into a room on the left and steered me toward one on the right. Cold fear spread over me as the space between us widened.

I found two police officers waiting for me behind a gray metal table. One of them was dressed in civilian clothes, and the other wore his police uniform. A single bare light bulb dangled from a wire, and on the table sat a pack of Marlboros. I knew from my Chinese friends that American cigarettes were in high demand, so I assumed that the officers meant the cigarettes as a friendly gesture.

The walls were concrete, and the room contained nothing but the metal table, a filing cabinet, an empty chair, and the cigarettes.

They shut the door.

I sat in the chair, and one of the officers pulled out a lighter. He politely urged a cigarette on me. I declined. Then the questions began:

"What brings you to China?"

"I came to study and to learn," I said.

"You like it here?"

"I like it very much. The Chinese people have been very friendly. I've learned a lot."

"Who got you job here in Beijing?"

"My friends and my colleagues at the company," I said. "I help during the day and teach a class in the afternoons."

"Do you have work permit?"

I wondered if that was the problem or if my friend had done something wrong in helping me secure the teaching job. I decided to answer simply and honestly, "No."

"What you teach them?"

"English."

"Teach anything else?"

"Grammar."

The officer shifted in his chair and leaned toward me.

"Who in the class ask questions about American government?"

My pulse ticked up a notch, and I thought about how to respond.

"Who in the class ask questions about freedom of speech?" the officer pressed, impatiently.

"I have different students on different days," I explained, carefully. "Many discussions about many subjects." It would be hard for me to say with certainty what any particular student had asked about any particular subject.

The room grew hot. I heard Han Lin crying across the hall, and I wished I could rush out to help her.

The officer in civilian clothes glared at me. I tried to reassure myself that I wasn't in danger. I was a nineteen-year-old kid in their eyes—not worth an international incident. But my friends had jobs they needed and dreams of going to America, and I didn't want to put those jobs or dreams in jeopardy.

"Why you teach English in this company?"

"What you do during day at company?"

"You have friend at company?"

The questions kept coming, and I tried my best to answer without jeopardizing my friends. Around midnight, I could feel myself getting fatigued. I said to the man dressed in civilian clothes, "It has been a pleasure speaking to you for two hours. I have done the best that I can in answering your questions. Now I think we should call the American embassy."

The officer pulled out a yellow softbound book with red writing on the cover. He ran his finger across several lines of Chinese text and then pointed at me. "You have broken the Chinese law. You *must* punish."

I held out my hands in a gesture that said I'd meant no harm.

Again he stabbed the page with his finger, his face growing ruddy. "You have broken the Chinese law. You *MUST* punish."

The air grew heavier as the gravity of the situation hit me. "I understand what you are saying," I told him. "And we can continue to talk, but I would like to call the American embassy, if possible."

In his broken English, the interrogator said to me, "If we must, but only to strike the Americans."

Was this a threat? Or was he having trouble with his English?

"I am so sorry, my friend," I said. "I don't understand exactly what you're saying."

"We can call American embassy, but only if you are hit."

That seemed like a bad deal.

The officer grew flustered. He was sweating and smoking and struggling with his English. Eventually, I understood that they'd only call the embassy if an American had been hit or injured in Beijing. They had no obligation to do so otherwise. I was in China. They were free to question me for as long as they liked.

I asked for water. They brought a glass, and we went back and forth a while longer. Finally, the questioning came to an end. They took my passport and explained that they would keep it until Monday, when I could return and pick it up.

I felt glad to leave but worried for Han Lin and my friends. Would they get in trouble for being in my class? Would they still be able to go to America one day? To my relief, Han Lin and my other friend were also released, and together we walked back to the dormitory. We tried to talk. I apologized to Han Lin. I thought this was my fault. She said she was embarrassed. She felt that she had been a bad host. I asked if everything was going to be okay. Han Lin said, "Yes," but she was exhausted, and so was I. We walked the rest of the way in silence.

On Monday I returned to the police station and paid a fine of roughly nine dollars. They made me sign a number of papers—all in Chinese—before I could take my passport. For all I knew, I could have been signing a receipt for the fine or declaring myself an enemy of the Chinese state. But I signed. I got my passport, and with the passport I could get home.

Several days later, I boarded a plane back to the United States. Security was different then, and inside my backpack I had the nunchucks, the kung fu sword, and—wrapped inside a pair of socks—the film canister with the photographs from Tiananmen Square. I also had a greater understanding of what those photographs meant, of the ideals for which those students had stood. I'd barely faced down two courteous police officers who'd been unlikely to harm me. Those kids—my age—had faced guns and tanks.

In security, they confiscated the weapons. A kind stewardess said, "I cannot allow you to bring these with you to your seat, but you can pick them up from me at the end of the trip." She gave them back when we landed. No one mentioned the film. Also tucked deep into my pack was the Australian outback adventure hat.

I left a lot of my naiveté in China. I also left a lot of my fear. I'd met ordinary people who'd acted heroically, and it now felt possible for me to do the same. On the flight home, I thought less about choosing an adventure and more about choosing a path with purpose. I began to think that I'd been born at the right time after all.

YOU: FIGHTING BACK

Earl tells you, "Now listen, baby, don't you go lookin' for trouble. Ain't no need for you to concern yourself with Ernest. Ain't no need for you to be anywhere near Clark Street. Kids always messin' 'round down there."

But Earl's not the one getting beat on, getting chased through the streets till he's scared to go outside during the day. Earl's so tough, not even a kid like Ernest would raise a hand to him.

You came to the gym because you wanted to learn how to fight, wanted to learn how to get strong so no one could pick on you ever again. You worked and worked and worked at it.

And you got good. You move fast now. You punch hard.

But that doesn't scare Ernest. He's always going to be older than you and bigger. He's always going to try to fool with you. No matter how hard you train, unless you show him with your fists, there's no way he's going to leave you alone.

Earl says, "You gotta be cool. Keep focused on what we're doing here. You got it in you to be a real good fighter. But not if you mess around with kids on the street like that. You gotta learn not to mind him."

You nod and you promise, but the day comes when you're alone on the street and here comes Ernest. He rolls right up on you, gets in your face. He pushes you.

The streets are empty. No one around to help you. No one around to stop you, either.

In your mind, Earl says, "Don't do it. Just walk away." But you feel a cold hard anger rise up in you. You think about all the times you've run away, scared. You think about all the beatings you've taken when you couldn't run.

You can take him. You know that. Two hits. That'll show him.

"Come on and do it," Ernest taunts you. He pushes you, knocking you back a couple of steps.

What do you do?

PUTTING ON THE GLOVES

I felt a bit of culture shock on returning to Durham, North Carolina, to the beautiful, contained environment of Duke University. I just kind of drifted from class to class. I remembered the lively discussions I'd had with students in Beijing and wanted to recapture that excitement.

I thought about my night at the Beijing police station, about the student who slipped me his film to smuggle out of the country. I thought about those who'd stood in Tiananmen Square, risking their lives for their ideals. As a student, I might not be able to change the world, but I knew I needed to live through something hard and real to become better. I wanted to challenge myself.

My grandfather Harold, whom I called "Shah," had grown up in Chicago during the Great Depression. He used to tell me stories about boxing there—the rough gyms, the hard poverty, the harsh discipline. His stories were full of all kinds of characters—righties and southpaws; big talkers and quiet, technical fighters; boxers and brawlers—and his admiration for all of them was clear.

I wanted to be like those men, who seemed to know how

to walk in the world—like my grandfather, who had served his country, raised a family, and had the confidence that came from being tested. The kind of confidence I'd seen in the student who stood, strong and grounded, as the *shifu* brought a sledgehammer down on the bricks stacked atop his head.

I couldn't do much with my sword and nunchucks, but I remembered Shah's stories, and I figured, *Why not test myself in the ring?*

So, on a balmy September evening my sophomore year, I pulled into the parking lot of the E. D. Mickle Neighborhood Center. Stepping out of my car, I kicked aside shards of brown beer bottles littering the ground. The gym stood in a rough section of Alston Avenue. Housing projects hung along the street, and men lingered at a gas station on the corner. This world felt very different from the tidy campus of Duke or the bustling streets of Beijing.

As I walked up the steps to the gym, I heard the sound of punch bags bouncing on their chains. Nervously, I pushed open the door, picturing a movie scene where all activity ceased and everyone stopped to stare at the newcomer. But the men inside barely glanced in my direction. No one spoke to me. I was the only white guy there.

The gym was one long room with a boxing ring at one end. Mirrors for shadowboxing lined the far wall. Three heavy bags hung from the ceiling, along with one speed bag behind the ring. In the middle of the gym, fighters skipped rope and trainers worked their boxers with punch mitts.

Trying to look like I knew what to do, I set my bag down

on a blue tumbling mat in a corner. I had no idea how to train as a boxer. I did a set of pushups until I got tired, and then I turned over and did a set of sit-ups. I had bought hand wraps from a local sporting goods store, and I stood and started to wrap my hands like I'd seen boxers do in movies.

A man walked up to me—muscled shoulders under a tank top, stubble on his chin, gloves slung over his shoulder. Unlike the *shifu* back in China, who seemed calm and unflappable, this man seemed coiled, ready to burst.

"Hey, man, you wanna spar?"

I imagined myself flat on the mat with a black eye. "No," I said.

He shook his head. "Man, how you gonna learn to box if you don't spar?"

I didn't have an answer for him.

I went over to the equipment closet and pulled on head-gear. I chose a pair of red gloves, yanked them on, and climbed into the ring. *Now what?* I wondered. *Do I just stand here? Shadowbox?*

My opponent stepped up the stairs to the ring and ducked between the ropes. He shuffled toward me, and I put my hands up, feeling lame and clumsy. He threw out a jab at my forehead. I swung back at him and missed, my gloved fist finding only air. He jabbed me high and then hit me low, right in the gut. He danced around the ring, smiling.

Frustrated, I ran at him, and he cracked me in the mouth. I threw another punch and missed. He tapped me with a right to the forehead, chuckling all the while. I felt the eyes of the other men in the gym on us, and I felt embarrassed and frustrated.

I kept running at him and missing. He kept dancing away, then moving in to land a punch. He could have knocked me out, but I wasn't worthy of that. I was just pathetic.

Eventually he'd had his fun and made his point. Without a word, he turned and walked out of the ring. Feeling defeated, I watched him go. I knew those men figured they'd never see me again.

ROUND TWO

When I went back to the gym the next day, the other men chuckled when they saw me, but they left me alone. I set my stuff in the same corner. *Okay,* I thought. *Let's try this again.* I did pushups and sit-ups until I was covered in sweat. I thought about skipping rope, but I didn't know how, so rather than do something that guaranteed I would look like a fool, I decided to punch a heavy bag, which only seemed *likely* to make me look like a fool.

For several days, I talked with no one, beyond "Hey" and "You done with that?" and "Yeah."

Finally, Bob Pugh—a former Southern Heavyweight Champion and the gym's manager—came up to me as I punched at a heavy bag.

"You're telegraphing your right."

I figured that was one of many things I was doing wrong, but I appreciated the tip. "How do I fix that?" I asked.

"You gotta get a trainer."

"Who's the best trainer?"

"Earl. Earl and Derrick."

"Are they here?" I asked, looking around.

"No, they're training outside the gym now, but I think I got Derrick's phone number."

Derrick Humphrey was twenty-six years old when we met for the first time at his apartment. He stood six foot two and had a scar across the bridge of his nose that I assumed came from boxing. Later, he told me that his mother had cracked him across the face with a wooden stick for acting up as a kid.

He also told me, after I'd known him for a while, that when I first called, he thought I was crazy.

"People call at least once a week, say they want to box," he told me. They were full of questions and interest for two or three days, and then they disappeared. "I could tell on the phone you were white," he said. "But when you said you went to Duke University and were spending your time at the gym, I didn't just *think* you were crazy—I *knew* you were crazy. But I like to keep my life interesting, so I told you to come on down."

Derrick introduced me to Earl Blair, his trainer. In the army they used to call Earl Bebop, because he walked with a bounce and a smile.

"How are you, how you doin'? So you're ready to fight?"

"Yes, sir," I said.

"Well, all right, then, all right."

Earl shook my hand hard. He was sixty-six years old, stocky, and strong. His smile filled his face, and he beamed with the joy of a man who seemed truly grateful for every day of his life.

"We talk money up front," Earl said. "Then there's no misunderstandings. It's twenty-five dollars a week. Paid on Monday. No excuses. Twenty-five a week, whether you train five days or none at all. Twenty-five a week."

I nodded and thought about how many lawns that would have meant mowing when I was a kid.

"Paying for something makes a man appreciate it more," he told me. "Learned that lesson when I used to train kids for free. Then they didn't have nothin' invested in it. Walk right on by the gym if they didn't feel like trainin'. When I first told Derrick, he wasn't sure he could pay. But have you missed one week, Derrick, in five years?"

Derrick grinned. He shook his head.

"No, sir. Prays on it. Works hard, and he gets what he needs. I always say, you might not always get what you want, but you always get what you need. I know my time is worth more than that. I'll get paid later, maybe in other ways. But it's important, all the same."

We walked into the parking lot outside Derrick's apartment. Kids on bikes weaved through the parking lot. Teenagers clustered in groups on the sidewalk. Music blared from radios, and cars honked in the street nearby. Every now and then, someone's mother would stick her head out a window and call a kid inside.

I looked at Derrick. *This* was the gym?

"Okay, now, here we go. Derrick and . . . and . . ." Earl searched for my name and came up empty. "And . . . and . . . both of you all, I want you to run. Gonna get those knees high. Ready. Time."

Derrick and I ran in place in the parking lot, lifting our knees high and punching our fists with every step.

Earl watched his stopwatch. "Time," he said.

Derrick walked a short circle around the parking lot, and I did the same.

"Got a beautiful day for training here," Earl said. "A beautiful day." We rested for what felt like thirty seconds, and then we did it again, running in place and punching the air. It seemed pretty easy to me, and I started to wonder if Earl was really that great a trainer. I also questioned how in the world Derrick could train for a professional boxing match by jogging in place in a parking lot.

We did a few more rounds, and then Earl said, "Okay, warm-up's over. Let's do it for real."

Derrick started pumping his knees and throwing his punches so fast that the kids on bikes stopped riding and stood watching with their mouths open. One boy got so excited, he started to imitate Derrick, throwing his fists as fast as he could.

I tried to match Derrick's speed, and just as I started to feel the burn in my legs, Earl said, "Time."

We stopped. Then we started again. Knees pumping, fists flying. It was exhausting and exhilarating at the same time. My body felt like it would give out any second, but somehow I kept finding energy for more. I'd never really pushed myself like this.

I started to think maybe Earl knew what he was doing.

"Time."

We took a break, then started again.

And again. And again. And again.

Kids circled us, and when I leaned over during one break and grabbed my knees, one of them said, "That white man's 'bout to pass out."

"You might be right, kid," I wanted to say, but just then Earl had us lie down on the ground, our backs against the asphalt.

I wanted to enjoy lying down for just one second, but Earl told us: "Get your heads up. Lift your feet off the ground."

We brought our heads up and our feet six inches above the ground.

"Hold it there," he said, and while I held my feet in the air, he walked over and punched me in the stomach.

Oof. My feet dropped to the ground, and I clutched my gut.

"Get your feet back up. You can take it. Watch Derrick." Earl strolled over to Derrick, who still had his feet six inches off the ground, and he started punching him in the stomach: *bam* with the right, *bam* with the left, *bam, bam, bam.* With each blow, I heard Derrick exhale and take another quick breath in through his nose. "Time," Earl said.

We worked out for hours that day in the parking lot. We didn't touch a single piece of equipment, and when I scraped my body off the pavement and dragged myself back to my car, I felt more beaten than I ever had after any practice, any race, any workout.

I couldn't wait to go back for more.

RINGSIDE

Before we started every practice, Earl made us pray. He'd tell us, "Just go on and say whatever is right for you to say," and we would shut our eyes and say a silent prayer.

I'd never spent time with someone who prayed on a daily basis, and it felt strange at first. But after a few days of getting regularly cracked in the ribs, praying seemed like a smart thing to do.

For Earl, any location where people gathered to make themselves better—the gym, the parking lot, or the patch of mud behind North Carolina Central University—was a place of worship. The ordinary tasks of boxing, like taping up our hands, were treated like solemn rituals.

My life felt split between two worlds, but somehow they came together. In the classroom, I'd learn about Aristotle, about his belief that we learn what is good by watching good people, and then I'd go down to the gym, and Earl would say to me, "Watch Derrick. Watch how he throws a jab."

So I learned by reading and writing and discussing, and I learned by watching and doing.

• • •

One day Earl told me I couldn't use the equipment in the gym closet anymore. It was time to buy my own.

"We all work on this bag here," he said, holding on to its battered form. "And when it finally break down, we each gonna put in to get a new one. Everything else, each one of my boxers has they own equipment. Own gloves, own rope, own hand wraps, own cup, own mouthpiece, own Vaseline. Why? Because I want to teach my babies to take care of what is theirs. Learn to 'preciate something. They take good care of those gloves, put Vaseline on 'em, put 'em out to dry when they get home, wash the strings. Compare that with them gloves and headgear they got in the closet there. Nobody pays that equipment no respect, none. But look here, go on, look around: every piece of equipment we got we keep it like brand new. Brand new. We're separate, and we're gonna keep it separate."

A few days later, Earl walked in carrying a cardboard box that said RINGSIDE BOXING in black letters on its side. He wore a big smile, and as he pulled out all my new gear—headgear, gloves, mouthpiece, boxing boots—I felt like I had arrived. I wasn't a boxer yet, but now I at least felt like a real student.

Because it was a big order, they threw in a few free items. When Earl pulled out a black ball cap that said RINGSIDE across the front, he took off his REAL MEN PRAY hat and pulled on the Ringside hat for himself. "Oh yeah," he said, grinning wide. "We got everything we need."

After our workout, I went into the locker room and took off my new gloves and my new hand wraps. I held my hands splayed in front of me and looked at my knuckles. The skin was torn from punching the heavy bag. Scar tissue would start to grow soon. But for now, I savored the blood on my hands, the cut on my lip, and the soreness in my jaw.

I looked in the mirror, not sure what I was expecting to find but feeling changed somehow, more myself. I squeezed my jaw and my cheeks and my nose, checking for soreness. I stood there awhile looking at my face. I thought about how unlikely a boxer I'd been on my first day, and about how now, I had begun to earn the strength that comes from working through pain.

It felt good.

A WRONG TURN

I asked Earl about the other boxers he'd trained. He told me a story or two about some of his favorites, but then he grew somber.

"Gonna tell you 'bout my first student, Beaver," he said, and I knew from the look on his face that it would be a hard story to tell. "Beaver had an older friend named Ernest. They grew up together, lived in the same neighborhood 'round Clark Street. When I first started training him, Beaver was in seventh grade and Ernest was in ninth. Beaver always felt he could never beat Ernest because Ernest was bigger. But after a few years of training Beaver, I told Ernest, 'I've trained Beaver. You can't beat him anymore.'

"But Ernest wouldn't take my word. He was gonna try Beaver anyway. Well, you know what happened. Beaver beat him up on the street. When I heard about it, I told Beaver, 'Why don't you leave Ernest alone? Stay away from him. You know he ain't no good.' I told him to stay off Clark Street, which was full of all kinds of mess. Kids makin' trouble.'"

Earl shook his head. "Next afternoon, I went out looking for Beaver to pick him up for practice. I saw a young man laying in the street, and I figured it was some man who got drunk and was laying out. Then I looked at his feet. *Those are Beaver's tennis shoes.* I jumped out my car.

"Ernest had shot him, and my baby's laying in the street, dying. I heard one of the kids say, 'Here come Earl,' but then I saw Ernest spinnin' tires, gettin' away, and I hopped in my car and went after Ernest, driving all over Henderson. He ran to the police station, but I think I should have stayed there and held my baby. Sometimes I think Beaver must've heard somebody say, 'Here come Earl,' and he probably thought everything was going to be all right. But I ran off after Ernest, and he died alone there in the street."

Tears collected in the corners of Earl's eyes.

"That's my regret. I just told him the day before, stay off of Clark Street. I told him, 'You know Ernest no damn good. Leave Ernest alone.' He was only eighteen. I had 'im hardly five years. My first student, my first baby."

Hearing Earl's pain, about his students, about the lives he'd lost along the way, made me want to work harder, to become someone great. I wanted to be part of a good story for him to tell.

UNOPPOSED

For three years, I trained with Derrick and Earl, and I learned as much about honor and discipline as I did about how to throw a jab. I learned that becoming good at something took a lot of hard work, and that every day you had to make a choice to show up and do your best. I learned that what you *did,* day after day, turned you into who you *were.*

My junior year, I wanted to box in the Golden Gloves tournament, but I fractured my leg playing football over Christmas break. That meant that the tournament in February of my senior year was my last chance to compete before graduation.

For weeks I ran in the early darkness of every morning, thought of boxing during the day, and slept hard at night. As Earl and I drove through a storm to Charlotte, North Carolina, to get to the tournament, my stomach was empty and my eyes were clear. I felt excited and a little nervous, but mostly I just felt ready. I'd spent three years sweating at the heavy bag, often until my knuckles bled. Three years of running and sparring, preparing for these fights, which—by the rules of amateur boxing—could last no longer than six minutes.

We parked the car and ran through gusts of snow and sleet

to make our way into the building. In the weigh-in room, we found a fat, sweating man sitting behind a table piled with USA Boxing amateur fight booklets and scattered bits of paper.

I introduced myself, and he squinted up at me.

"Oh yeah, yeah, from up in Durham. You called me a few times, didn't you? Well, let's get you weighed in."

"One fifty-six." The upper limit for light middleweight. I had hit my weight exactly. I felt pumped and ready for my first Golden Gloves fight.

"Beautiful," Earl said, and clapped me on the back.

"Oh, good. We need somebody at Novice Light Middleweight. With this storm, we've had all kinds of guys cancel. We'll be lucky to have twelve fights. Half the card's going to be unopposed. Can't remember last time we had weather like this."

Earl said, "Who's our opponent?"

"Well, we don't have one right now in Novice."

My gut sank with disappointment. I looked at Earl.

"We want to fight," Earl said.

"Well, we want you to fight, too. But you need an opponent."

He told us to wait until registration closed. I went upstairs to prepare, and Earl joined me after a bit. As he walked over to me, he held up a piece of paper that had my name listed in the "BLUE CORNER" column next to "156 NOVICE." I was fighting "UNOPPOSED."

I looked down at my gym bag and the small cooler at my

feet. I felt ridiculous for having made such careful preparations. I had prepared for three years and driven through a snowstorm to get here. And now I couldn't fight?

Earl and I watched a few matches. I kept looking around the room, hoping my opponent would make a last-minute appearance.

Finally, they called me into the ring and handed me a trophy. I turned away from the scattershot applause and hurried out. As we walked through the lobby, I held the trophy limply, upside down. It felt like a joke.

"Hold on," Earl called after me. We stopped in the lobby, and he turned me to face him. "Now, look here, Eric. You are the Golden Gloves Novice Champion. You earned that trophy. Now, go on and hold it right."

"Earl," I started to protest. I was mad and embarrassed, and I didn't want a life lesson just then.

But he kept going. "You been workin' hard three years now. Real hard. And you can box. You did everythin' you needed to do and more. That there trophy's goin' up on the mantel. Right for everybody to see. Baby, all we can do is do right. That's all we can do. And you've done that. Everything else is up to my Father. You know how to fight. Look at all the guys you beat in the gym. You been workin' hard. You earned it."

"Yeah, but I wanted to fight for it," I said.

Earl put his hand on my shoulder. "I know you did, baby."

One evening a pro fighter named Maurice, known as Mo "Too Sweet," came down to the track where Derrick and I sparred.

Mo was a professional fighter. He did his road work on the track at Central, and sometimes he'd come down to work the bag with us.

"I got a match coming up in a few weeks, and I've been looking for someone good to spar with," he told Earl. "Can I work with Derrick?"

"How about Eric?"

Mo cast a skeptical look my way. "Eric?"

Earl said, "Eric's no joke. Plus, he's closer to your weight."

"Eric, huh? All right." Mo smiled. "I'll be sure to take it easy on him."

I'd seen Mo fight and win at the Ritz in Raleigh. He was a talented professional fighter—fast and strong. I thought to myself, *Earl's lost his mind.* But after the Golden Gloves disappointment, I wanted a fight.

Earl set down orange cones to carve out a ring on the track. Mo and I touched gloves, and we were off. I was used to fighting Derrick, who had a much longer reach. Mo was shorter than I was, and so I was able to close with him easily. I jabbed and felt the full force of my punch crack against his face. His head snapped back, and I had to keep from grinning. It was probably the best punch I'd ever thrown. I followed Mo around our makeshift ring, and I kept jabbing and the jabs kept cracking.

As he slid around the ring, I realized, *He's running from me.* I hit him, and he cracked me back hard. Our sparring grew in intensity. I threw a right that knocked him on the side of the head, and he stumbled. I pursued him, moving fast and strong, fluid and instinctual. My years of training were paying off. Mo turned and unloaded a right hand full of malice that flew past my head. We weren't sparring anymore. We were fighting.

Earl had been working with me on throwing a right hook to the body followed by a right hook to the head. I jabbed first, then shot my fist into Mo's ribs, and with a twist through the hips, I turned the punch over and brought my fist barreling over Mo's low left hand to smash his temple. The impact shot through my whole body.

Mo stumbled again, then turned his back on me and walked out of the boundary of the ring.

"I told you Eric could fight," Earl said.

Derrick added, "Eric, I thought you were 'bout to kill Mo in there. You got yourself a little fight in you now."

That night Earl called me. "Need you to come over the house. Come when you can." And he hung up.

It sounded urgent, so I rushed over to his place. He hustled me through to his dining room. On the table a rectangle of gold-colored metal lay next to my Golden Gloves trophy. Earl picked up the piece of metal and handed it to me. Engraved across it: ERIC GREITENS. I held the piece of metal and felt oddly formal knowing that Earl had used my last name.

"Now," Earl said, before I could ask any questions, "turn that over. See that piece a tape, that backing there? Take it off."

"Okay."

"Now, press it right into that marble part. Right below the man."

I pressed my name into the trophy, right below the golden figurine.

"It looks like you, the way you fought Mo. How's it sticking?" Earl asked.

I smiled. "It's good."

"All right, well, you take that on home with you. See you tomorrow night if the Lord spares me."

"Thank you, Earl."

On the way back to my apartment, I glanced over at my trophy and smiled. I loved Earl. I was still disappointed about the Golden Gloves tournament, but I'd earned something even more important: strength, discipline, and the respect of a wise man.

YOU: HELPING HAND

Places like this freak you out. You hate the smell — urine and antiseptic. You hate the feeling of sadness that settles over you the minute you walk through the door. But you love your grandfather, and that's why you're here. To see him — possibly for the last time — before you go off for months to another country.

You feel a little guilty, as you pass by room after room, trying not to glance through open doorways at the men and women lying there, mouths open, TVs droning in competition with one another. Your grandfather loved to travel more than just about anything. Now his travels are behind him while yours stretch ahead. You tell yourself he's happy for you and admires what you're doing. You just hope you can make him proud.

He lies propped on the bed. His face is the color of ash, and though he still has his pot belly, his arms and legs look thinner to you, depleted. He smiles when he sees you, though it only registers on one side of his face. When he takes your hand, though, his grip is strong.

His lips are always chapped now, probably because he

can't easily sip water on his own. You stopped on the way for a tube of lip balm, which you take out, remove the cap, and hand to him. He can't speak, but you can see he's grateful.

He raises the tube to his lips, his hands trembling, but he can't quite get it to work. The lip balm hovers an inch above his face. He puckers his lips and tries again. Still, he can't control his hand well enough to do it.

You feel stuck in place, numb. You want to reach out and help him, take the tube from his hands and apply the ointment to his parched lips. It's a simple thing, but you're frozen. All of your life, he's been strong and independent. You don't want to take that from him. But you don't want him to suffer, either.

You stand there, watching him struggle. You feel awkward, unable to bridge that small distance.

He drops his hand, and the tube of lip balm rolls onto the blanket in front of him. All you have to do is pick it up, touch it to his lips. Pick it up and help him.

What do you do?

LAST GOODBYE

In the summer of 1994, when I was twenty years old, I volunteered to go to Croatia to work with the Project for Unaccompanied Children in Exile. I had read about the brutal conflict between those who wanted to create an independent Bosnian state and those who wanted Bosnia to remain part of Yugoslavia. Each day the news ran images of people fleeing burning homes, families trapped in cities under siege, women who'd been assaulted, and children orphaned by terrible acts of violence during campaigns of ethnic cleaning. It didn't feel like enough to sit and talk about the situation. I felt pulled to do something, to help in whatever way I could, even if that just meant bringing comfort to a handful of people.

Along with several other students, I had raised money to cover our expenses. We intended to live and work in refugee camps in Croatia to help the children and families who'd survived the ravages of the conflict.

Before I left on my trip, though, I stopped into the nursing home where my grandfather Shah lived after suffering a second debilitating stroke. Shah had always been a hero to me; his stories about boxing fueled my passion for the sport, and he always seemed so vigorous, so knowledgeable, so much larger than life.

He was also a talker, so much so that his nickname came — as family legend said — from my trying to tell him, as a kid, to "shush."

For the last eight years of his life, after my grandmother died, my grandfather had been on his own. He'd filled his time with travel and study, and told me wonderful stories about his experiences. Shah had gone to Mexico to take a class on art and had visited the museums in Mexico City. He came to see us in St. Louis and took classes at the local community college. He always seemed to be searching, always seemed driven to explore, learn. I wanted to be like him, someone who embraced life.

At one point, after his second stroke, he had to be fed through a tube connected to his stomach because he couldn't swallow. By then he was unable to speak. During one of our visits, he shakily scratched out a note that read, "Don't let them starve me."

Down but not out, like the old fighter he was.

On my last visit to see Shah, I went to the nursing home alone. I wanted a few private minutes with the man who had inspired me, even if we couldn't really talk together.

I'd stopped on my way to buy him a tube of lip balm, knowing his lips were often dry and cracked. When I arrived, he lay in bed, looking smaller and more fragile than I'd ever seen him. His brisk vitality was gone. His face was slack and gray.

I put one hand on his shoulder, and he took my other in his, giving it a good squeeze. He had a little fight left in him still. I handed him the lip balm, and he grasped it lightly. He focused his eyes and pursed his lips. He lifted the tube to his face and tried to apply it, but the tube wavered an inch away and the balm never touched his lips.

Paralyzed by sadness, I stood there and watched him. The effort tired him, and he set his hand back down. I should have reached across, taken the lip balm from him, and helped him apply it. But I didn't. Something held me back. Fear, probably, and inexperience with caretaking. My mind told me to reach across those few inches to help him, but I couldn't make myself do it. I watched as he struggled.

I've looked back many times since that moment, always disappointed with myself. I was motivated to fly across an ocean for adventure and to do a good deed, but at the same time I was incapable of providing a simple helping hand to my own flesh and blood.

It was the last time I saw my grandfather alive.

SMASHING BOTTLES

I'd taken a semester of Bosnian, but I found the language difficult. On the train from Vienna, I proudly used the one complete sentence I knew in the language: "*Ja sam u vlaku za Zagreb.*" (I am on the train to Zagreb.) How that was supposed to carry me through weeks of work in refugee camps, I had no idea, but if I were ever again on a train to Zagreb, I could let people know.

On the train a middle-aged Bosnian woman wearing jeans, a rumpled jacket, and thick-framed brown glasses heard my accent and stopped me in the passageway between cars.

"Are you an American?"

"Yes."

She asked me where I was going and where I came from in America. I told her, and she said, "Why isn't America doing anything?"

"Doing what?"

"Why isn't America doing anything to stop the ethnic cleansing, to stop the rapes, to stop the murders? Do you know what is happening to the people of Bosnia? You know what's happening. Now, why don't you do anything about it?"

I had no answer. I tried to explain that I was here to help.

"If you're going to help, why don't you *do* anything?" Her hands trembled, and her mouth pressed into a frown. She added, "You'd help us if we had oil."

I walked past her and stood at the window of the train. I felt uncertain again, as I had in that nursing home with my grandfather. We had crossed into Croatia, and I got my first look at the vivid green hills and squat white homes that dotted the Croatian countryside. A red compact car drove along the road parallel to the train tracks. I raised my hand to the open window and waved. The man riding in the passenger side of the car stuck his hand out the window and flipped me off.

When I got to the Puntizela refugee camp, kids came running toward us. They looked like any group of American schoolchildren. Most wore clothes that had been donated by Americans or Europeans, and as they clustered around us, I felt surprised at how clean they were, how seemingly well-fed and happy. The refugees I'd seen on the news always looked dirty and distraught—lost in misery.

The kids jostled us, asking, "Have bonbons?" or "Have chocolate?" Those who couldn't speak English simply opened their hands or scrunched the tips of their fingers together and touched their lips to signal for treats. I felt dumb for not bringing any.

Two boys grabbed my hand. I thought they wanted to hold it, but they turned my wrist over. They wanted to look at my watch.

Another boy ran circles around us as we walked toward the camp. One of the boys looked at him and then back at me. He frowned, shook his head, and rolled his eyes in the international sign for "That one's nuts."

Behind the kids followed Dario and Jasna. A married couple and refugees themselves, they ran the volunteer projects in the camp. Dario was a barrel-chested guy with black hair and a face covered in stubble. Beneath the stubble, his smile was full of joy but twisted just enough at the corner of his mouth to make you think he was about to fire off a sarcastic bullet.

I reached to shake his hand.

"Hey, how are you doing? Welcome to paradise," he said with a chuckle. He spoke to the kids in Bosnian and then told us, "The kids love you already, and they'll keep loving you as long as they think you've got candy."

Jasna had dirty-blond hair and a meek but warm smile. She walked behind Dario and barely said a word. Later I'd learn that her English wasn't great, but she managed to convey a wicked sense of humor. She was the more practical of the pair, making sure the volunteers had a place to stay and that they knew the work schedule. She told us when lunch would be served. They made a good team: Dario kept everyone's spirits up, and Jasna kept the camp running.

The Puntizela camp stood outside Pula, Croatia, a beautiful city that was home to Roman ruins, including the Arena, one of the largest amphitheaters in the world. The stone walls of the ancient structure still towered 106 feet in the air, providing shade for the ice cream vendors who set up shop on the stone streets. The refugee camp was set in a park on the edge of the

Adriatic Sea. Bright blue water glistened off a rocky beach, and tall cypress trees surrounded the area.

The refugee families lived in trailers. They were cramped, but given my expectations about the misery of refugee life, I was surprised to find families living in trailers at a seaside resort.

I threw myself into life at the camp. I started a soccer team with one of the refugee boys, helped in the kindergarten, played chess with the teenagers, and talked with the adults. I sat in trailers with families and drank endless cups of coffee. I thought about the distance between this camp and the classrooms at Duke — the distance between talking and *doing*. My days rushed by.

I knew just enough Bosnian phrases, and could utter them with enough conviction, to give the false impression that I actually knew what I was saying. Often I'd sit for long periods understanding little as my hosts took long drags on their cigarettes and exhaled a flurry of words and smoke while animatedly chopping the air with their hands. I tried to nod at appropriate moments.

Sometimes one of the refugees who spoke good English — often a teenager who would roll his eyes because the old men were repeating themselves — would translate the conversation for me in dollops.

"Then the Serbs came to his house. He told them to go away, but . . ."

"And now he is talking more about his cousin . . ."

"Still more about his cousin. He was, like, twenty-eight years old."

The beautiful setting of Puntizela couldn't hide the reality of what had happened to these people. I heard stories of horrific violence. Although I knew that Dario and Jasna were refugees, I didn't actually connect the word to violence until they told me they came from Banja Luka.

In 1992, when the war broke out, the Serbian army took control of the city, hanging white rags on door frames to mark Bosnian homes. Soldiers stormed these homes to take dishes, televisions, furniture, jewelry—whatever they wanted. Serbian soldiers beat old men with the butts of their rifles, smashed fingers with crowbars, and dismembered bodies with their knives. They raped women and girls. They shot or slit the throats of anyone who resisted.[2]

The Serb soldiers rounded up Bosnian men, women, and children and took them to concentration camps like Manjača. They identified the community leaders and took them elsewhere to be beaten and tortured. Some of these people "disappeared," never to be seen again.[3] Many of the families I met, victims of the ethnic cleansing, had been forced to grab what they could and walk away from their homes. Often the buses packed with refugees were diverted to killing fields.

I thought about my grandfather, about how he had fought in World War II, about how the world had vowed to "never again" allow genocide. Yet these atrocities kept unfolding.

In cities and towns across Bosnia, the Serbian army forced men, women, and children into mosques and held them there for days. Sometimes they threw them a few bits of bread or gave them a couple ounces of water. Prisoners were forced to go to the bathroom on the floor of the sacred mosque where many of them had prayed and worshiped nearly every day of their lives. After starving them for days, the soldiers "offered" pork to the Bosnian Muslims and asked them to denounce the teachings of the Qur'an.[4]

I found these details so sickening, I couldn't believe that the people sitting in the trailers telling me these stories were the same people who had lived them. The stories seemed to come from another world entirely.

A man in one of the camp shelters told me that his wife had been dragged from their house and raped. Both of his brothers had been killed. His sister and parents had been living in a different city, and he had no idea if they were alive or dead.

He lifted his shirt to show me the scar on his stomach and chest left by a grenade that had been thrown into his house. He considered himself lucky that his children and wife were alive. He started to cry. I looked at his children—a boy and a girl who sat together in the corner. I felt grateful they had survived, but more than that, I felt a strong desire to help them and others like them.

One night the refugees gathered for a party in a common area that sometimes served as a classroom. Music played, and everyone drank beer. After a while some of the teenagers started to throw the empty beer bottles on the concrete floor, and shards of glass soon littered the room.

One drunken kid hung on my shoulder and said, "Don't be scared. This is Bosnian tradition. We drink this s—t beer and party in this s—t place."

Many of the older refugees left. One boy cranked up the music and yelled something I didn't understand, and then two boys smashed into each other like they were in a mosh pit and started to wrestle standing on the glass-covered floor. More bottles smashed on the concrete.

I felt their anger and frustration, their need to release some of the pent-up energy that came from being confined in a strange place, their whole lives turned upside down through no fault of their own.

I could also see that these teens struggled more than anyone in the camp. The adults who were parents and grandparents could keep busy taking care of the children, and they found purpose in that love and that work. The younger children were generally resilient, as kids are. But the war had hit these teens just as their real lives should have begun. While some found purpose in helping care for others, most led aimless lives. They were trapped in the refugee camp with no prospects for a job, no prospects for further education. They had limited opportunities for fun, few chances at marriage. In their situation, I might have been smashing bottles myself.

DIPLOMACY

On many nights I sat in the common room as a radio played and the refugees talked and played chess. Denis, fifteen years old, was one of my frequent chess opponents. He wore jeans and a donated T-shirt, and often had a cigarette hanging from his lips. As we played, he would ask me questions about America, questions about where I had traveled, about my education.

Every time I asked him a question, he laughed and shook his head. He didn't want to talk about his life, and I couldn't ask him the kinds of questions I'd ask any average American kid: What subjects do you like in school? Do you have a girlfriend? What do you like to do on the weekend? Denis had no school, no girlfriend, no way to think about a future beyond the camp.

I'd play chess for hours. I was a weak player, and even the eleven-year-olds sought me out. One young boy always sat and stared at me across the board. He played on the soccer team that I'd started, and chess was his chance to turn the tables and coach me. After each one of his moves, he would watch as I analyzed the board. When I took too long, he would roll a short circle in the air with his hand: "Okay, okay."

A moment came in every game when he would begin to shake his head, as if he had hoped that maybe this time I'd have provided some real competition. Disappointed, he would put me into checkmate.

To muster my pride, I'd remind the eleven-year-old, "Well, I'll see you on the soccer field tomorrow."

"Okay, okay."

Once I brought a bottle of vitamins to soccer practice. With all the boys standing in a line, I handed out a "vitamin for athletes." Using a combination of English, Bosnian, and charades, I told them that these would make their muscles grow.

A kid—nine or ten years-old—gave me a look and yelled, "Those are the vitamins from the kindergarten!"

"Yes," I said. "But the kindergartners can't do the exercises to make their muscles strong. If you take the vitamin *and* do pull-ups, you'll grow strong."

I never knew what kind of impact I was making, so one day I felt great when I saw an older man in a wheelchair roll himself out to watch our soccer game. Soon others came out with blankets. They smoked and talked and clapped as they watched the kids play. The game became an afternoon ritual.

One afternoon, however, almost none of our fans showed. Had I done something to offend them?

I asked the man in the wheelchair, but my Bosnian and his English couldn't connect. I asked one of the kids, and he said, "They are watching *Dallas*."

"The TV show?"

"Yes." Every day, I learned, the women of the camp crowded

around a tiny black-and-white television to watch episodes of the American show, broadcast—I believe—from Italy. I wondered what these people who'd lost their homes, who crowded into trailers and had no idea what their lives held in store, thought of the greedy and materialistic Americans portrayed on TV.

Living in the refugee camp put things in perspective, but even there I remember losing sight of how hard this life was on the people around me. Walking back to my trailer with another volunteer after lunch one day, I complained about the food: the same hot mush again. Gently, she suggested that my problems paled next to the refugees'. I felt ashamed of how self-centered I was being. The hot mush was sustenance for these people who could no longer cook in their own homes or make their own decisions about what to eat. I vowed to keep my grumblings to myself and not to take the comforts of my life for granted.

After several weeks, I moved on to work in a second refugee camp. This one, Gasinci, was more like what I'd imagined a refugee camp to be. Hundreds of prefabricated shelters had been laid out in straight lines like a military encampment. Where the families in Puntizela seemed to all know each other, this camp was crowded with refugees, many of whom were strangers to one another. Volunteers from various relief organizations were also packed into the camp. People seemed to overflow from every structure. This was no seaside resort.

My first morning in Gasinci, I startled awake to the sound

of exploding artillery. I shot straight up in bed and smacked my head against the upper bunk. The Croatian army regularly conducted maneuvers on a hill near the camp, and eventually I got used to the sound.

Even though the Croats and Bosnians had forged an alliance against the Serbs, hostilities remained between the sides who'd previously fought against each other, and that resentment spilled over into the camp. A few days into my stay, Croatian soldiers shot two puppies that the kids in the kindergarten adored. The whole camp was in an uproar over the incident, especially those from the United Nations, whose role was to protect the refugees.

I watched as outraged workers for the High Commissioner for Refugees debated what to do. In the end, they decided to write a letter. Watching them work on it—not fifty yards from where the puppies had been shot in full view of the kids—I realized that the UN workers had very little real power. They only brought in aid when the people with guns allowed them to.

Later, when I thought about the UN workers in Gasinci writing their letter, when I read about what had happened in the town of Srebrenica—where more than eight thousand people, mostly men and boys, were slaughtered after the Dutch UN troops allowed the Serbians to enter a formerly "protected" village—I realized that there was a great dividing line between all of the speeches, protests, good wishes, and words in the world, and the one thing that mattered most: the ability to protect people. In situations like this, good intentions and heartfelt wishes were not enough. The great dividing line between words and results was courageous action. And sometimes that action meant the use of force.

Sitting in Gasinci, watching the tumult over the drafting of a letter, I finally understood the anger of the woman who had approached me on the train: "Why don't you *do* anything?" Something in me shifted, and I felt a different answer stirring. I still wanted to help those who'd been hurt and oppressed. But I also wanted to go beyond that, to become not just a help to people after they'd been hurt, but part of a force that could offer strong protection in the first place.

From that point on, I tried in my own small way to be protective. In Gasinci, a director of one of the nonprofits asked if we could bring all of the kids outside to meet a donor that afternoon.

"Why?" I asked.

"The donor wants to throw out gum to the kids, and I would like you to make photographs."

I could imagine the scene: a donor surrounded by children, tossing out gum like he was throwing feed to animals in a zoo. "Why doesn't the donor sit down with the kids and talk to them?" I asked. "They can show him what they've been working on. I'll take photos of that."

"Yes, but they want photos of the donor handing out gum."

You wouldn't walk into an elementary school recess in America and start tossing out gum and taking photos of "desperate children." So why here? These kids were smart and creative. They were survivors who deserved better.

Many of the aid organization advertisements for refugee

children made the kids look as pitiful as possible—dirty, hungry, begging. The children I worked with in the Gasinci camp did need help, but they also needed their dignity.

I didn't want any part of it. "I won't take those photographs."

"But you must."

"Actually, no. I don't must." I walked away.

In the shelters, I listened as old men smoked and argued about the future. Occasionally, someone would translate, but I couldn't follow the conversation very well. The smoke was heavy. Once, I cracked the window an inch and stuck my nose out just to get a whiff of fresh air. The men laughed at me. But the conversation was serious. One man shouted and gestured wildly at the others nearby. He believed that all the young Bosnian men living there should be out fighting.

I sat with a man who pointed at the roof of his hut and told me he appreciated the shelter and the bread. He pointed to his children at play and said he appreciated the volunteers and the crayons and the schoolwork. "But," he said, "we need the Serbs to stop burning villages and raping women and killing brothers."

Again it struck me that helping these people was not the same as protecting them. Providing for those ravaged by war was not the same as stopping those who'd brutalized them.

Before I left Zagreb, I called home.

"Hello," my mom said, and I knew from her voice that my grandfather had died. I sank into a chair and waited for the bad news. When she actually got the words out, she started to cry. "I thought he would wait for you to come home."

I finished the call and set the phone down. I thought of my grandfather's stories, about his love of adventure, about how I'd found boxing because of him. Then I remembered my last moments with Shah. I could have guided his hand an inch lower to touch the lip balm to his mouth. That's all it would have taken. Here I was in a foreign country, out to save the world from genocide, and I hadn't even had the courage to reach over the bedside to help my grandfather.

PROTECT FROM HARM

When I returned to Duke at the end of the summer, a friend invited me to speak at a local church. "We want to know what's happening in Bosnia," she told me. That seemed like much too enormous a topic for me to do justice to, but I agreed to go.

On a Sunday afternoon, I stood at the front of a room before some twenty people seated in metal folding chairs. One of the congregants introduced me, saying, "We've all read in the newspaper about what's happening in Bosnia, but you're the first person any of us have heard from who's actually been there."

I pressed the forward button on the slide projector, and a picture appeared on the screen of a girl drawing a house on the ground with a chalky rock. I thought of all the children who'd still found ways to laugh and play even when their lives had been devastated.

The photos were mostly of individual children and families living in the two refugee camps where I'd worked. I pressed the button again—*click-clack, click-clack*—and showed a picture of refugees stepping off the bus into Gasinci.

"So many of these people have lost friends and family

members," I said. "They have no idea when or if they'll ever go back home."

Click-clack, click-clack.

"This boy's mother was killed in Bosnia . . ."

Click-clack, click-clack.

"This is where all the kids went for classes . . ."

Click-clack, click-clack.

"These are the shelters where refugees lived in the camp."

With each turn of the carousel, I felt the attention of those watching grow sharper. I could see that for the first time, the members of this church had connected on a human level to what they saw and heard about in the news. When they read about thousands of people driven from their homes, it was abstract. When they saw one family dragging a bag across a field in search of shelter, they understood.

Looking at it through their eyes made me see it differently, too. It made me grateful for my love of photography, and for my desire to be on the ground and to interact with real people. I'd gone there and lived with these refugees, shared meals, played chess and soccer, and sometimes laughed with them. Every photograph had a story I remembered.

When I finished showing the photographs, the lights flickered back on, and I offered to take questions.

A white-haired gentleman raised his hand and in a dignified Carolina accent asked, "This may seem silly, but where did they get their food when they were in the refugee camps?"

The questions continued like this.

"Where did they get their clothes? How did they wash their clothes?"

"What happened to the rest of the girl's family?"

The people in the church wanted to know not about an issue, but about the daily lives of other human beings.

The photographs and video footage that appeared on TV often captured moments of incredible tragedy: women wailing, children bleeding. The photographs I showed were of people who were very much alive, some of them smiling. These people didn't just see a little Bosnian girl drawing a picture of a home. They saw a little girl who could have been their daughter or granddaughter.

One of the church members asked, "Why did the Serbians want to kill these people?"

Before I'd left for Croatia, I would have had at least a partial answer to the question. I would have described the abstract conditions that led to the massacres—the rise of nationalist politics and ethnic tensions, the weak response of the United States and the United Nations.

But having lived in the refugee camps, I was, I think, a bit wiser. I said, "I don't really know *why,* any more than I know why any human being ever abuses or tortures or kills any other human being."

The final question came from an elderly lady sitting in the back row. She asked, "What can we do?"

Such a simple question, and one that I should have anticipated, but it caught me off-guard. I could have told her to send used clothing and toys overseas, or to donate money to organizations that helped refugees. But I remembered the anger of the woman I met on the train from Vienna who'd asked, *Why isn't America doing anything?* And the words of the refugee in Gasinci—*We need the Serbs to stop burning villages and raping women and killing brothers*—echoed in my head.

For a long moment, I didn't know what to say, and grew uncomfortably aware of the audience looking to me for an answer.

Finally, I said, "We can certainly donate money and clothing, and we can volunteer in the refugee camps. But in the end, these acts of kindness come after the fact. After people have been killed, their homes burned, their lives destroyed. Yes, the clothing, the bread, the school—all of it helps and is very much appreciated. But I suppose we have to behave the way we would if any person—our kids, our sisters, brothers, parents—were threatened. If we really care about these people, we have to be willing to protect them from harm."

YOU: TAKING RESPONSIBILITY

Your parents are dead. All of your family is gone. It is always hot, and there is much illness, especially among the little children. Always, your belly seems to rumble its emptiness. And even here, adults steal from one another, fight, sometimes kill.

But you've learned what you need to do to survive. You've created a shelter for yourself. You are healthier than so many others. You grab food and water when it's given out, hiding some away for when the supply runs dry.

One day, as you lie in the shadows beneath the blue tarp that stands between you and the blazing sun, you hear a sound. You roll over and press your hands against your ears. But the sound reaches you still. A little child—crying.

Sighing, you rise and leave the comfort of the shade. In front of your shelter stand two little boys. They are barely clothed, and tears leave shining trails in the dust on their faces.

"Go away," you tell them. "Go to your people."

But they stand there, mouths open like baby birds, crying and scared.

You want to throw rocks at them, make them run away. You can only take care of yourself. No one else.

Yet they are so little. Their arms look like twigs ready to snap.

You could take them into your shelter and share what little you have. You could help dry their tears, give them sips of water, make sure they are not injured. But you have yourself to worry about too. Everything you give to them is something you take from yourself. If you don't offer, they might find help elsewhere or they might die.

The sun beats down hard. They stand and look at you.

You could yell at them, scare them away. Or you could stand aside and let them in.

What do you do?

FRESH EYES

In the days that followed my time in Croatia, I felt like my path
had become more clear. My life was crystallizing around one
idea: serving. I wanted to be on the ground, on the frontlines,
to help other people directly. I didn't want just to talk about
world politics in an abstract way. I wanted to get my hands
dirty, to act and hope that my actions would make a difference.

My love of photography provided a way to do that. I could
go and help people, and I could also document their lives,
bringing their stories back to share with others the way I had
in my friend's church.

One of my professors, Neil Boothby, had organized the
work I'd done with Bosnian refugees. In May 1995, the summer before my senior year, he invited me to join him on another trip — this time to Rwanda, a place that a year before had
become synonymous with death and chaos. I knew about the
events, about how the assassination of the Rwandan president
had set off an explosion of violence between two groups — the
Hutu and the Tutsi — that resulted in a devastating hundred-
day campaign of mass murder and genocide.

I conjured images I'd seen of rivers choked with the bloated bodies of the dead, piles of human corpses so massive that they'd used bulldozers to push the dead into massive open-pit graves. Try as I might, though, I couldn't wrap my mind around the idea of almost a million people being slaughtered. I thought about what it would be like if one out of every eight people I knew had been killed. I wondered how it felt to exist in a country where such brutality had so recently unfolded and what it would be like to travel there and try to help those who had survived.

I bounced in my seat as we drove along the rutted dirt road to Kigali, the capital of Rwanda. For at least the seventh time, I patted my lucky shirt—a pale safari-style shirt that I'd worn in China and Croatia—to check that my passport, money, and ticket home remained hidden and safe.

Two boys in tattered shirts ran barefoot along the road beside us—the bigger boy chasing the smaller one with a stick. A rickety roadside stand offered cigarettes, phone cards, and cookies and crackers. Its owner, a reedy man who stood barefoot in oversize black pants and a red button-down shirt, raised his hand in a halfhearted gesture to flag us down. A boy soldier with an AK-47 strapped over his right shoulder fixed unfriendly eyes on the UN vehicle and then on Neil. I tried to imagine a boy soldier on the streets of an American city, and I couldn't picture it.

Neil had moved his family to Rwanda after the UN had appointed him senior director of programs for the orphaned and abandoned children of the genocide. These children were referred to as "unaccompanied." It struck me how inadequate this language was to communicate the horrors that deprived these kids of their parents and family.

En route, we passed the gates of the Hôtel des Mille Collines.

"During the genocide, that hotel was a haven for refugees," Neil told me.

The manager of the hotel, Paul Rusesabagina, had saved more than twelve hundred lives during the brutal days of the attacks, a story later made famous by the movie *Hotel Rwanda*. Paul would one day become a friend, but at the time I didn't even know his name.

Neil directed the driver: *"Tournez à gauche."* (Turn left.)

We turned down a side street and pulled into the United Nations compound. It stood on the grounds of an old elementary school, now converted into offices for aid workers. UN peacekeepers from India, listless and dressed in sloppy fatigues, opened the gate.

I thought about my elementary school, and it made me sad to think that this school in Rwanda was also once a place of learning and fun. Now its rooms were dedicated to people who came to help those who suffered in war.

Inside, Neil showed me his spare office—little more than a table and metal chair in an old classroom—and introduced me to a few of the other international aid workers. They all dressed in hiking boots, cargo pants, and safari shirts. Books written in a dozen different languages peeked out from their deep cargo pockets. The entire world, it seemed, had sent men and women to help—but only after the slaughter of almost a million people in a few short months.

I put my anger aside and stayed focused on my purpose. Neil and his colleagues wanted to determine which of the UN-backed relief efforts were most effective. Where were they doing real good, and where could they do better?

Neil had given me a simple mission: accompany UN aid workers and other humanitarian personnel to visit the sites of aid projects throughout Rwanda and neighboring Zaire. Look. Listen. Ask questions. Take photographs. Take notes. Then report back.

I was not—as many who'd come to Rwanda to help were—an academic researcher or an anthropologist. I wasn't a social worker. I wasn't a nurse or a doctor. With only one summer of experience with Bosnian refugees under my twenty-one-year-old belt, I was an expert in nothing. But in a way, this gave me advantages.

I came into the situation unencumbered by prejudice and expectations. I came with fresh eyes and could ask simple questions:

"If the aid workers have access to two four-by-four trucks, shouldn't they be bringing health services out to the villagers rather than having sick families and kids walk miles to the health clinic? Why don't we drive from village to village and bring the equipment and doctors directly to the people who need them? Wouldn't that allow us to serve more people, especially the ones who are too sick to get here on their own?"

There were often good reasons for doing things a certain way, but sometimes my questions pointed to flaws in the system, as well as to human weaknesses: corruption, vice, laziness.

It also helped that I was a volunteer. I had paid for my own plane ticket and my few expenses with documentary photography grants, so no one owned my time. I was willing to travel long distances in cramped trucks to visit remote projects. What I lacked in knowledge, I tried to make up for with energy.

HOMECOMING

One day an aid worker named Jill grabbed me for a mission. A small woman with delicate features and short black hair, she spoke rapidly and had a laugh that spilled out fast and switched off abruptly.

As I jumped into the truck, she told me, "We're going to monitor a repatriation. These are refugees who fled and are now crossing back from Tanzania into Rwanda."

"How many are coming across?" I asked, imagining the courage it took to return to a place you'd fled in fear for your life.

"Maybe a hundred, maybe two hundred. We never really know until we get there."

At the border, I watched refugees stream back into Rwanda. Over the men's shoulders hung burlap sacks and plastic bags filled with their possessions. They sweated under their loads, many of them dressed in jackets. The things they carried, the clothes on their backs, represented all they had left.

The women carried children in their arms or wrapped tightly against their backs. They wore cloth head wraps, on top of which sat misshapen bags full of clothes, pans and jugs, keepsakes, and other objects. Young girls carried their infant siblings. I saw a piece of black Samsonite luggage being dragged on its last stubborn wheel across the stony dirt as the refugees made their way to a UN water truck.

I began photographing children as they went to fill their jugs. Intrigued by my camera, the kids posed and played in front of it, showing off with their fists in the air and their arms draped about each other. I laughed with them as they clowned, feeling lighter at the small expressions of innocence and joy. A girl smiled under a wide-brimmed umbrella, its yellow and red panels faded by the sun.

I focused my lens to take the girl's picture, but someone gripped my arm and turned me roughly. A man with an AK-47 slung over his shoulder grabbed my camera. Without thinking, I yanked it back. The soldier was two inches shorter than I was, and I could tell from his effort to take my camera that he was weak. I could also tell from his eyes that he was scared.

He pointed at my camera and shook his head, saying, "No. No," as he reached for it again. I turned my shoulder toward him and pulled the camera back.

"Okay, okay," I said, putting my hand on his shoulder in what I really hoped would be considered a friendly gesture.

"No photo."

"Okay," I repeated.

"No." Once again he grabbed for my camera.

When I pivoted away from him, he turned his palm up and flexed his fingers in the universal symbol for "Give it to me."

I wasn't going to give up my camera. It had become an extension of me, a way of connecting to and preserving the stories of the people I met, the places I traveled. More than that, it was my way of bringing their stories home.

"Okay," I said, reluctantly, hoping I'd come upon a decent compromise. "I'll give you my film."

I hit the rewind button on the camera. As the film started to spool, his eyes shot from me to the camera and back again. Was I playing some trick on him?

He stood there under his black beret, sweating through his fatigues. I popped the film out of the camera and handed the roll to him. He took the film, and I saw relief wash over him. Sweat dotting his brow, he said, "Yes," and walked away.

My muscles slowly unknotted as Jill and I watched dozens of families straggle across the border. They filled their jugs at the water truck and boarded a bus that the UN had chartered to take them into Rwanda. They packed into the bus, four and five people per bench, bags of belongings piled on their laps and in the aisles, off to see what remained of the places they had abandoned months ago. Would their homes still be standing? Would other families be living there? Where would they sleep tonight?

I admired these families and their will to keep going. I wondered how I'd fare if my neighbors and loved ones were killed, if I was driven from my home and returned to find everything gone. How would I feel? Would I be able to keep going?

In my mind, every step these people took testified to their strength of character. Back in my college philosophy classes, we'd talked about courage. It had many definitions, but here I got to see it in its purest form: you did what had to be done, day after day, and you never quit.

A PICTURE'S WORTH

Rwanda seemed both full of shadows and full of beauty to me. On our way to the health care clinic, we passed fruit fields, and I'd smell tea leaves and the sweetness of newly ripened bananas. Coffee bushes burst with ruby-red berries. Thin farmers swung hoes to claw at the brown earth of the terraced hillside.

Early in the morning, the place took on a mystical quality as fog clung to the hills. To the southeast, the forests supported thirteen species of primates and hundreds of species of birds that rose every morning with the sun.[5] It seemed tragic that such a beautiful country had become synonymous with such ugly acts.

Yet the images of refugee camps and border crossings that flooded the media told only part of the story. The news sells tragedy, but often misses stories of strength. It left an impression of desperate, downtrodden, despairing people. But there, as a small part of things, I got to see so much more.

At the clinic, I saw dozens of women and children sitting in the grass talking under the high sun. Many of these women had walked for miles with their children, hoping to get bandages and antibiotics. They had carried children with earaches and blurred vision. There were other families, however, whose children seemed healthy and playful. When I asked one woman why she'd come to the clinic, she said, "So my son can play and also to talk to the doctor."

Another women asked, "You have children?"

"No," I said, "I don't have any children." That felt like a long way off to me, but I realized some of these mothers were my age or younger.

"Your children are beautiful," I added. She translated this to her friends, and they all smiled.

I sat down in the grass with them. The day felt calm, wide open, and for a few moments as I sat there under the high sun and watched the children run and play, I felt like I was at a kid's birthday party in a park. At any minute, someone might bring out a cake.

A middle-aged woman with her hair wound atop her head sat down next to me. A Rwandan aid worker, she had an air of gravity, and the other women turned their eyes toward her. I later found out that she had raised five children and was a former schoolteacher. She was a survivor of the genocide, but her husband had been killed.

She smiled encouragingly at the women, who began to speak. When she responded, she moved her hands in the air like she was conducting a symphony. The women told the stories of their survival, which the aid worker translated to me in snatches of detail and dialogue.

They talked about fleeing for their lives, running with their children into the forest to escape the thugs. A woman with a deep, ugly gash on her arm from a machete attack told the aid worker, "They mistook me for dead and threw me into a pile of corpses." She'd waited all night until the Interahamwe — members of the death squads who'd brutally raped and hacked their fellow countrymen to death — fell into drunken sleep in the early morning. Only then did she run away.[6]

Other details rose from the group:

"A woman I played with as a child had a son who joined the Interahamwe and became a murderer."

"She ran out of her house, but her sister was behind her, and they caught her and they raped and killed her that afternoon."

I struggled with taking photographs that day. I wanted to capture their portraits, to share what I saw with others. These women had suffered more than I could imagine, and still they welcomed me, told me their stories.

And yet I hesitated to use my camera. If I tried to take photos, I'd be asking to take a piece of each person who had suffered and share their story with strangers. As I sat debating, one woman sitting before me propped up her young child on his two wobbly legs and encouraged me to take his photograph.

She smiled at me and laughed. When I raised my camera, I looked through the viewfinder and saw a whole group of women smiling back at me.

Driving back to Kigali, I thought about what I was trying to do. Some people had spent years serving in Rwanda. I was going to be here for six weeks. How was I supposed to contribute? I decided I could at least take photographs like the ones I had just snapped. I could give Americans a glimpse of Rwandan lives, with all of their facets: joy, loss, strength, hardship, compassion.

WELCOME TO ZAIRE

Nervously, I stood in the customs inspection line to cross from Rwanda to Zaire. I'd been warned about how dangerous it was in the refugee camps in Zaire. Some of the Hutu refugees there had killed and incited others to kill during the genocide. Rumors swirled that these refugees were using the camps to regroup and rearm. Some said the French government financed weapons for them. Other rumors implicated priests in the Catholic Church.

I had no idea if any of that was true, but before me stood a man dressed as a priest in a gray suit with a white clerical collar. He lifted a brown satchel onto the inspection table, his body language tranquil.

The young customs agent unsnapped a silver buckle and pulled the sides of the satchel open. His eyes grew wide. Gingerly putting his hand in the bag, he pulled out a pile of American hundred-dollar bills. I'd never seen such piles of money—stacks of hundreds bound together crisply with rubber bands. The priest had to be carrying, it seemed, at least forty thousand dollars.

I wondered where he'd gotten it and, more than that, how he intended to spend it.

After the satchel had been checked and the money re-packed, the priest secured his bag and walked into Zaire, his stride cool, his expression unflustered.

My hiking backpack held a few shirts, film, pens, and note-books. I passed quickly through customs and headed down the twenty yards of dusty road separating Rwanda from Zaire.

As I crossed the border, I ducked under the arm of a traffic gate. A man sitting on a rickety chair next to a card table stuck out his hand. I gave him my passport.

He looked it over and surveyed me with dull eyes. "Do you have a visa?"

"No, I'm sorry, I don't have a visa."

Shaking his head, he told me, "You must go back to Rwanda to get a visa."

"Where in Rwanda?"

"In Kigali."

I'd been told that fifty bucks would get me across the bor-der. I didn't know if the fee was legitimate or an established bribe.

"I thought I could get my paperwork taken care of here."

"Well, it is difficult to do, but it is possible."

"I understand that the fee is fifty dollars, or perhaps you could accept this from me as a thank-you for your help and an apology for the inconvenience I've caused."

"Yes, no problem, sir."

Using a mangled pen, I scratched my name on a sheet of

white "entry point" paper. The official took the paper, spun in his seat, and lifted a rock from atop a stack of stained forms. He put the sheet of paper I had just signed on top and replaced the rock. Welcome to Zaire.

A military jeep came barreling toward me, dust swirling, and ground to a stop. A soldier in a black T-shirt and black beret stood in back, aiming a mounted machine gun at my chest. My nerves sparked, but I forced myself to stand still.

He spat words at me and pointed to a flag being raised behind the customs hut. A scratchy recording of music played in the background. I recognized it as an anthem and relaxed a bit. Now I understood. There was a flag-raising ceremony. I needed to pay my respects.

I stood straight and looked at the flag. Out of the corner of my eye, I watched a bead of sweat trickle down the sharp plane of the soldier's face. He narrowed his eyes at me. The gun still pointed at my chest, his right index finger an inch from the trigger. Once the flag was raised, the soldier shouted at the driver, the vehicle barreled away, and I stepped with shaking legs into the customs hut.

The soldier inside reeked of alcohol. He pointed to the floor, and I dropped my bag. After unzipping my backpack and pushing my clothes around, he stood and looked at me with glazed, bloodshot eyes. Thrusting his hand under my nose, he rubbed his thumb against his other four fingers. He wanted money. When I just stared dumbly, he made a fist, thumb out, and tilted his head back to mime drinking. He wanted alcohol.

I shook my head. "No, I don't have any alcohol."

He made the money and drinking motions again. Again I played dumb.

Three other soldiers carrying AK-47s entered the hut. I stiffened. Every detail of their postures, their weapons, stood out in sharp relief.

Neil had warned me about aid workers who'd been shot and killed in Zaire. I imagined having to wrestle a rifle from one of them. Who would I grab? How? What chance did I have against four armed men?

I sized up the distance between me and the exit, and one of the soldiers moved to block my path. I knew they intended to rob me of something, and my mind raced through the possibilities: how I might bribe, how I might escape.

A Land Rover four-by-four pulled up outside the customs hut, and out jumped a white woman with blond hair the size of Texas and an even bigger smile. Before I'd heard her say a word, I knew: *American.*

She carried a bag of cookies in one hand and a carton of apple juice in the other. As soon as she said, "Howdy, y'all," to the Zairean soldiers, I knew I was safe.

She handed out the juice and cookies—"Y'all be good now"—and the soldiers smiled back. I grabbed my bag and jumped in the truck, and we took off down the road.

COMMITTED TO A MISSION

Goma, Zaire, was home to the largest of the refugee camps surrounding Rwanda. Some 1.2 million survivors stayed packed together in an area with unhygienic latrines and muddy water, a scarcity of food, and an abundance of disease.

When the refugees had first settled in Goma, a cholera epidemic swept through the camp, hastening thousands to their deaths. Refugees hiked for miles to chop down trees for cooking fires, stripping the forests around Goma bare. They built shelters of rocks and sticks that they covered with the blue tarps provided by the United Nations. They filled these rocky hovel homes with donated blankets on which lay their often-sick children, while the adults waited in long lines for food distributed by international aid organizations.

Legions of workers from large and small relief organizations buzzed about the camp. I arrived there months after the first refugees had established temporary homes, but the camp still had no central organization.

The Red Cross had put up a large wooden board nailed to poles dug in the ground. Families and aid workers posted pictures of missing children and of those found living alone in the camp.

Though the Office of the United Nations High Commissioner for Refugees was supposed to be in charge, they had little power. At night the camp often turned violent as old scores were settled, and as the sun fell, most of the aid workers drove out of the camp to houses nearby, where they slept behind high walls protected by armed guards.

The UN workers came from around the world. Most had good intentions, but some seemed motivated by the attractive Western salaries, schools for their children, and homes in Nairobi. The most intensely motivated volunteers—those who worked twelve to fourteen hours a day for little or no pay—were mostly American Evangelical Christians.

They began every day, every meeting, and every meal in prayer. They were absolutely committed to saving souls and saving lives, and they worked with a feverish intensity, as if the day of reckoning might come at the end of the week. They had attempted to learn the language; many understood the culture; and they made real friends among the refugees.

At their worst, some of the Evangelicals could be insensitive to the feelings and experiences of the men and women around them. One day, as I photographed an outdoor church service in Goma, Karen—the blond woman who had been my savior at the border—stood to preach. A refugee translated as she spoke.

Karen lectured the crowd of genocide survivors who sat on rocks under the high sun: "If you do not make Jesus Christ your personal savior, you will go to hell." Lifting a book from her chair, she held it out to demonstrate. "It is a law, like the law of gravity." She released the book, and it thudded on the platform. "It is a law. Accept Jesus, or spend an eternity in hell."

I looked around at her makeshift congregation, who smiled and nodded at the words of the translator. Afterward I asked a man what he thought of her sermon.

His answer came back to me: "She had a beautiful message."

"Tell me what she said."

"She said we cannot always carry everything on our own," the man explained through the interpreter. "If we try, we will drop things. We must ask for God's help to carry our burdens." Apparently, the translator had taken some liberties with Karen's sermon.

She and her friends were sometimes out of touch, but they also rose every day with the sun and spent hours tending to the needs of sick children, ordering supplies, distributing food, and reuniting families. They may have been culturally clumsy, but each day I came to admire them more for one simple reason: they were here in Rwanda. They were working. I was visiting for weeks. They had committed themselves for months.

I thought back to the discussions I'd been a part of in my college classes, and I imagined some of my classmates rolling their eyes at these earnest volunteers. But none of those intellectual debates had ever saved a life, while these committed people spent their days weighing infants, providing food to nursing mothers, and generally trying to lighten the load of those who'd been cast from their homes with nothing.

Much of the international aid I saw could have been more

helpful. Some of it was even harmful. But the world would be a colder and darker place without the people who worked to provide it. Whatever her flaws, Karen was feeding hungry families every day.

THIS ONE IS POWERFUL

A young Rwandan man who volunteered with Food for the Hungry asked me to accompany him into camp. He led me to a group of boys whose "home" consisted of nothing more than long sticks covered with pieces of black plastic and blue tarp. They slept on bare earth, which in Goma was black, jagged volcanic rock so hard and barren that weeds could hardly grow.

In the dark tight space where the back wall of the shelter angled to meet the ground, a boy lay curled up. He couldn't have been more than eight years old. I motioned for him, and he crawled out of the shadow of the shelter, dragging one foot behind him. An ugly open wound marked his ankle. As I bent to examine it, the sickly sweet odor of infected flesh assaulted my nose. He needed care, urgently.

"Where is the nearest medical tent?" I asked.

The volunteer pointed. "It's over there, but it is a long way."

One of the boys spoke to the volunteer, and he translated: "The boys say that they went to the tent before but were told to leave."

Anger flared in me. Why would anyone have turned this boy away? "They won't tell me to leave," I said.

I hoisted the boy into my arms and started to carry him over the rocky ground. His companions followed, chattering away at the volunteer.

"The boys say that they were told not to come back."

"That's okay," I said. "No one told me." This boy would receive care if I had to grab supplies and do it myself.

The bright Red Cross symbol announced that we'd come to the right place. I carried the boy into the white tent, where I found three nurses sitting on plastic chairs and talking. One cot held an old man whose open, lifeless eyes suggested he'd come there to die. I watched his stomach rise and fall against a brown T-shirt pocked with holes. I set the boy down, and he hopped on one foot toward the nurse.

I prepared for a battle, but the nurse—herself a refugee who had been hired by the Red Cross—took one look at the wound and sucked air in through her teeth. She showed the infected ankle to the other nurses, they conferred, and she reached for a bag of cotton balls and bottles of alcohol and iodine.

She held his leg, her hands sheathed in blue latex gloves, and as she dabbed around the wound, the boy's skin shone as layers of dirt washed away. She wrapped his ankle in a clean white bandage and patted his knee.

I wanted to ask why he'd been turned away before, but all of the nurses had been incredibly kind, and I didn't want my words to be mistranslated. I thanked them, and we walked out of the tent.

The boy hobbled back to his friends, and by the time we reached his shelter, his friends were gathered outside and singing. They bounced on bare feet, their smiles wide, elated. I imagined some of them feared that their friend would die, like so many others whose wounds became infected and went untreated. They danced around me and sang a joyful song.

The Rwandan aid worker whispered, "They are singing 'thank you' for what you did."

I was barely able to force a smile. I felt sick inside. As an American, I had paid an insignificant bribe at the border, was bailed out with apple juice and cookies, and could walk unchallenged into any part of the camp I wished. These boys had survived unimaginable horrors to arrive here and now could not get the most basic help.

"Tell the boys 'thank you' for their song," I said to the aid worker. "And ask if I can talk with them."

They gathered closer, and he said, "Yes, yes, they wish to know who you are."

I pulled a pack of St. Louis Cardinals stickers from the pocket of my cargo pants. "Please tell them these are from my home in America." I handed out the stickers and then sat down. The boys sat with me.

I learned that the oldest was sixteen and had become the leader of this group of boys who lived together in the refugee camp. They were all "unaccompanied," and they looked at me with eyes far wiser than those of most American children. They could be playful, but they held their shoulders back with an air of self-possession rare among children I'd known. It was like sitting with young soldiers. When I smiled at them, all fifteen faces smiled back.

The leader wore a ragged T-shirt and a pair of donated

shorts. I asked him to tell me about the other boys in his group. One by one, he pointed to his friends, describing them for me as the aid worker interpreted.

"This one is very powerful with making fire and cooking." He pointed to another. "This one is very powerful with the soldiers from Zaire; they like him." He moved his finger. "This one is very powerful with singing." It may have been some quirk of the translation, but as he went around the group, the leader described each boy as powerful in some way.[7]

The international community had stood by and watched the genocide in Rwanda. It had taken a military victory—a Tutsi army that swept down from Uganda—to bring an end to the killing. We should have sent military assistance. Instead, too late, we sent money and food.

As I left Rwanda, I thought of the way parents love their children. They hug them when they need love, care for them when they're sick, heal them when they're injured. But parents also protect their children when they're threatened. Good parents don't hug their children, tend to their wounds, but then leave them to be assaulted.

Nations are not parents to the world's people. Yet the basic fact remains: we live in a world marked by violence, and if we want to protect others, we sometimes have to be willing to fight.

We have no choice but to go forward in the knowledge that it is within our power, and that the world requires of us—of every one of us—that we be both good *and* strong in order to love and protect. I felt I had done some good in Rwanda, but I knew I had more to learn and far more to do.

YOU: CAPTURING DEATH

It's not that death is new for you. You've traveled to other places and seen famine, disease, and violence. You've seen piles of human remains from brutal attacks, and you've seen the lone dead, borne off by illness and starvation.

But this is different. This is a little boy, and his death is so pointless and so poignant that you feel urged to capture it, to imbue his death with some kind of meaning. You want to share with the world what you've seen in the hopes that it will someday stop happening.

The only way you know how to do that is to take a photograph. You know that your camera can say much more than your words can. You know that showing this little boy to others might move them to act, to volunteer their time, invest resources that might keep other children like him from meeting the same fate.

And yet this is a funeral. His body lies in its little casket, and it feels wrong to just snap a picture of him. It feels disrespectful to him and to his family. This is their private grief, even though the whole community is participating in it.

Your camera bumps against you as you move closer, its

weight insistent. You run your hand along the curves of the lens, and you consider.

One image, just one, and you might move people to open their eyes, to help. One image, just one, and you might make a bad day worse for these mourning people.

What do you do?

BAZOOKA JOE

By the time I stood under the sun with a group of friends at graduation in May 1996, I had been given the greatest gift an education could provide: I had a better idea of what it meant to live a good life and what it meant to be a good person.

Duke's parting gift to me took the form of another photography grant that paid for a plane ticket to Santa Cruz, Bolivia, to document the lives of children living in the streets there. Maybe it was the fact that I wasn't so long out of adolescence myself, or maybe I just felt protective of those who were younger and less fortunate. Whatever the reason, I was moved to take this journey. As I filled my backpack with film, camera, notebooks, and some well-worn travel clothes, I took pride in the fact that for a kid who'd never been far from Missouri when I left for college, I'd covered more miles in the last few years than I'd ever imagined I would.

In Croatia and Rwanda, I'd photographed the remains of the dead and listened to the stories of survivors. I'd seen people — even amid incredible tragedy — continue to care for their children and one another. I saw people rebuild their lives in small steps, one arm wrapped around their neighbors for support. Despite all the suffering I had seen I left these places feeling hopeful. I found that volunteers could save lives and bring joy. Bolivia would prove to be a different kind of test.

Commonly referred to as *niños de la calle*—children of the street—the homeless kids in Santa Cruz spend their days shining shoes, begging, and selling gum and cigarettes. Some of them return to small cardboard or corrugated metal shelters to sleep at night, usually in groups and often surrounded by dogs for warmth and protection. The children live in alleys, their shelters in shadow.

Some children end up on the street after being abandoned. Others flee abusive homes—and wind up in a place of equal, or worse, violence. Young women, in particular, are often the victims of sexual abuse. Cutting—self-mutilation—is common among these children.

Sniffing glue is also common. Some children lift small white bottles of chemicals to their noses a hundred times a day. For them, it's a reflex, like blinking. The cheap drug eases pain, makes them forget their circumstances for just a few moments. But it also causes brain damage. Seizures, spasms, memory and hearing loss are also common.

Once, I watched a young girl—maybe seventeen years old —tilt a bottle to her nose and breathe in deeply. Her eyes were wet and glassy as she set the bottle down on her pregnant belly. I gritted my teeth at the damage she was doing to herself and to the baby inside her, but I also wondered how cheap her life must have felt to her, if the moments of forgetfulness were the few bearable ones she had.

A woman I'd met at Duke told me about Mano Amiga—a

home for children of the street run by two of her friends. She described it as an oasis of joy in the desert of poverty, abuse, crime, and destitution where most street children lived, and she described her friends as the closest thing she knew to living saints. I knew I wanted to spend time there, to learn and help serve in whatever way I could.

The Mano Amiga home was located just outside Santa Cruz — an hour's walk from the center of the city for a barefoot child. My first night there, I gathered with the volunteers and all of the kids in a large room that also served as the dining hall. Here I'd eat simple breakfasts, lunches, and dinners of bread, stew, and vegetables served from steaming black pots.

A hulking man stepped into the room. Linebacker big, he had black hair, olive skin, and small glasses that gave him a professorial air. A deep, soft voice gave his words a feeling of pastoral reverence.

In Spanish he said, "Welcome, everyone. My name is Don Thomas. I have been working in and overseeing these homes for years and with great pride and happiness."

I called up every bit of Spanish I'd learned in high school and college so that I could understand him.

"Every time I introduce new volunteers . . ." I lost some of his words but understood when he said, "I feel truly blessed that you are here." He smiled broadly. "The work you do here is not only a great contribution to the children of Bolivia but also a great contribution to all the children of God. On behalf of everyone here" — and he opened his arms to take in all of the children — "thank you for coming. Now, let us all introduce ourselves."

We first heard from Jason and Caroline, the young American couple who ran the home. Jason was a Wisconsin native who approached every task — attending to wounds, refereeing conflicts — with the unhurried pace of a Midwesterner walking out to his barn. His wife, Caroline, equaled him in intelligence and compassion. She could gently discipline a child, rattle off instructions in Spanish about how lunch should be served, switch to English to tell a volunteer where to find art supplies, and pick up a crying kid from the floor. And she did it all with an easy smile.

"I talked to my sister on the phone," she told me once, "and for her birthday, her boyfriend got her a diamond necklace." She smiled. "For my birthday, Jason gave me a back rub."

The smile wasn't rueful. It didn't seem for one moment that she'd prefer the necklace. Their work at the home afforded them no material luxuries, but it seemed to provide the best kind of happiness: simple, deep, and true. I remember thinking, *What a beautiful way to start a marriage.*

Then the children introduced themselves: Rodrigo, Carlos, Adolpho, Maribella. One after another, they stood — as shy, as silly, as earnest as any group of American kids. I leaned forward in my chair, straining to understand them. Many had come from rural villages surrounding the city, and their native language was Quechua. I'd been looking forward to using my Spanish and had totally forgotten that they might speak other languages instead.

One boy — maybe six years old — stood and shouted, "I am Eddie!" and flung his arms to the side, as if he were a rocket shooting through space. He posed dramatically, clearly expecting our full attention. I smiled as he flopped back down on his chair, though after another couple of introductions, he lifted off again, bounding around the room, curling his arms like a monkey, scratching his armpits and grunting. I struggled not to laugh.

"Eddie," Caroline said simply, and Eddie returned to his seat with a grin.

I decided to introduce myself using the Spanish name I'd been given in my high school Spanish class, thinking it might be easier for the kids to pronounce than Eric. But when I stood and said, *"Hola, me llamo Quí Qué,"* the kids burst out laughing. Even Don Thomas chuckled.

Was my Spanish that bad?

Two of the kids chanted, *"¡Quí Qué chiclé, Quí Qué chiclé!"* and mayhem ensued.

Embarrassed, I turned to Caroline, who explained that in Bolivia, Quí Qué is a popular brand of gum. My introduction was the equivalent of a Bolivian volunteer announcing to a group of Americans, "Hello, my name is Bazooka Joe!" Later the kids walked up to me, puffing out their cheeks like chipmunks, pretending they were chewing impossibly large wads of gum.

A NEW NORMAL

I "kicked off" my first day at Mano Amiga with a lesson in the Bolivian national religion: soccer. Jason and I walked out to a dirt field beside the home, where a pack of boys, some barefoot, kicked around a ragged brown ball. Some of the boys wore donated shoes; some had outgrown their shoes and had cut holes in them, playing soccer with their big toes hanging out.

Alone, people can feel hunger. Alone, we can feel pain. To feel poor, I realized, we have to compare ourselves to others. In Mano Amiga, these kids weren't poor. Their recreation consisted of soccer, tag, a dozen other run-and-chase games, marbles in the dirt, bottle caps. Using their imaginations, they turned old tires into fighter planes and cardboard boxes into candy stores.

I took off my shoes and raced alongside the others. It reminded me of soccer games in Croatia and I thought about how, no matter the circumstances, kids all over the world feel the urge to play.

José, one of the volunteers, would often roll in the grass with the boys, wrestling playfully with them. Many of these kids had experienced the physical strength of adult men only in the form of abuse. José taught them to control their strength. He never hurt them, and he didn't allow them to hurt others.

Although the refugee children I'd worked with in Rwanda and Croatia had lived through incredible, sometimes vicious trauma, most had an otherwise whole life with loving parents or other caring adults. While the refugee children suffered greatly, there was a good "normal" they might return to one day. But "normal" for many of Bolivia's street children meant abuse and violence sewn into the fabric of their days from the moment they were born.

Every night Jason and I had to round up the boys and get them into the showers. Like kids everywhere, many of the boys in the home didn't care about being clean. Jason made a game of it. He'd announce, "Shower time! *¡Vamos, vamos, vamos!*" We'd stomp after them like boogie monsters and chase the kids into the showers.

One night Adolpho was covered in dirt from soccer and had crumbs of food on his face and crushed into his hair. He didn't want to shower. Jason had tried the boogie monster chase. He tried making it a challenge—"Adolpho, let's see how fast you can shower and get to bed." He tried to reason with him—"Adolpho, I'd feel really happy if you got clean and into bed."

Still, Adolpho refused.

"Adolpho, please, you need to shower and go to bed," I said, and gently grasped his wrist. The moment I made the lightest contact with him, he fell to the floor and screamed—a full-throated scream that filled the hall with the sound of his terror. Arms and legs flailing, he writhed on the floor, shocking me and those around us.

I had two younger brothers and three younger cousins. I'd seen plenty of kids throw tantrums. But I'd never seen this. This was the wild fear of a child who'd known abuse.

I felt awful about adding to his trauma. I lowered myself to the floor next to him, not touching him but letting him know I was nearby. Calmly, I said, "Adolpho, relax. You're okay, relax. You're okay."

Slowly, he quieted, got to his feet, and padded off to the shower.

Adolpho had to build a new normal.

CREATING BEAUTY

I took my camera into the poor neighborhoods of Santa Cruz. I told myself that I took pictures so I could share stories with others. Maybe, too, the act of photographing people and their surroundings made me feel safer, less awkward. To photograph gave me a purpose beyond mere curiosity.

I turned off the paved main streets onto narrow, muddy paths. The acrid smells of rotting trash and urine rose in the air as I wound my way through a maze of hovels where ragged clothes hung on sagging laundry lines.

Brown runoff trickled between the houses, bearing plastic bottles past discarded rags. If every crumpled plastic bag littering the ground had been a vegetable, it would have been a bountiful garden. It struck me that these people had so little, and yet trash seemed abundant.

I thought back to the evening I'd spent with Bruce Carl in that homeless shelter, about how strange it had felt to sit with those men and listen to their stories. Now, years later, I'd become more accustomed to squalor and deprivation, but Bruce's challenge remained: to find a way to listen and to learn about the lives of others.

On either side of me, mud-caked walls and rusted corru-
gated steel roofs formed homes the size of one-car garages.
Waved inside by an elderly woman, I entered one of the homes.
I felt more like an intruder than an invited guest.

Inside, I saw an immaculate dirt floor. A sheet hung from
the metal roof to divide the cramped space into two rooms.
On one side of the sheet, well-worn blankets provided a bed.
Farther back sat a small iron stove for cooking. A small crucifix
stood tacked to the wall above the stove, and an image of the
Virgin Mary presided over the door frame. Outside, kids ran
barefoot, splashing through puddles of standing water.

When the children turned to me, I saw bright smiles under lazy eyes. I saw elbows and knees with open sores. I knew
that the kids ate what their caretakers scrounged for them or
whatever they could steal or buy with a day's earnings from
working on the street. Throughout Bolivia, kids without access to clean water and sanitation died needlessly from malaria,
hepatitis A, and toxic chemicals in polluted water. I also knew
these children lacked access to even the most basic health care
to set a broken bone or kill intestinal parasites.

Back on the streets, I passed packs of boys shining shoes,
and a little girl—maybe eight years old—selling gum from a
box that hung from a strap over her shoulders.

"*¿Chiclé?*" she asked.

I bought the gum and kept walking.

At night I would go with a group of Americans who gathered in the city, sang songs to embolden their spirits, and then
walked down the small dirt paths to where children of the

street lived. They brought with them bandages, hot tea, and bread.

We saw children lounging together in packs—their arms draped over each other, glue bottles in their hands. A boy stood next to a Dumpster reading a newspaper, casually lifting a bottle of glue to his nose with his free hand. The children drank the tea and accepted the bread. I had expected them to be voracious, but they chewed slowly, their eyes darting left and right as they ate. Most of them were high.

The volunteers bandaged wounds, using rubbing alcohol to clear away layers of grime. They replaced brown rotten bandages with fresh white ones that seemed to glow against the children's unwashed limbs. Sometimes the kids responded when we handed them tea, and some smiled at my camera, but I'd never walked among children like these, children who seemed so much like zombies, their brains wrecked by drugs, the light of their spirits barely flickering under years of daily pain and abuse.

As I walked home one night, I found myself breathing shallowly in and out of my nose like I was preparing to fight. My body felt tense.

What's the matter with me?

At first I thought I was angry about the street children, angry about their plights. But I soon realized that my anger was selfish. I wanted to see—as I had in Croatia and Rwanda—cause for hope. I wanted to believe that the situations of these children could be improved, their lives saved, their wounds healed.

But on these streets, I found little to hope for. Many of these kids were too far gone. Drugs had rotted their brains, and a dozen or more years of bad habits locked them into cycles of misery and addiction. Miracles were possible, but it seemed that *only* a miracle could help kids in this corner of the world.

In the Mano Amiga home, though, it felt different.

"Here," Caroline explained at the beginning of a lesson, "we teach art—music, painting and sculpture, and dance."

Eddie ran by, holding a paper plate that had been glued with construction-paper arms and legs and a head to make a monkey—his favorite animal.

"Why do you teach so much art?" I asked. "Why not just basic reading and writing? Or math?" I loved the arts and loved seeing these kids work so earnestly on their crafts, but when I remembered the squalor outside, it felt smarter and more practical to give them skills they could convert into productive lives.

"I want them to see that there are beautiful things in the world," she told me. "And that they can create them."

Kids like Adolpho and Eddie were incredibly intelligent. Some had survived for years on the streets, and I often saw in their narrowed gazes an emotional maturity that far exceeded that of most American children. Yet these kids had never had someone who believed in them enough, loved them enough, to teach them that *they* had value, that *they* could create beautiful things in the world. They had never learned what they were capable of. Until now. It was a small spark of hope.

KEEPING FAITH

In the Mano Amiga home, we played a game that the volunteers called — in a mash-up of English and Spanish — the Sniffing of the Manos. Before we let the kids enter the dining hall for meals, they had to line up and hold their hands out, palms up. The volunteers would then inspect each pair of hands to see if they'd been washed.

Carlos, a bright-eyed ten-year-old, held out his hands. I sniffed, then scrunched my face as if I smelled something rotten.

Carlos and the other kids around him giggled.

"Good. You pass." Carlos danced into the dining room.

I sniffed Pablo's hands. Putting a pensive look on my face, I stroked my chin and began the interrogation in my simple Spanish.

"Tell me, did you wash your hands with soap?"

Pablo giggled. "Yes, Quí Qué. I did."

"And how long did you wash your hands?"

"Twenty seconds, like you told us."

"Are you sure it wasn't nineteen seconds? Because if it's

nineteen seconds, you'll have to go back to wash your hands again."

He rolled his eyes, grinning. "Yes, Quí Qué."

"How fast were you counting?"

"Real slow. *Slow . . . like . . . this.*" He drew out each word. "Okay."

Pablo shot a crazy face at the other kids and ran into the dining room.

Two places down the line, Adolpho stood and fidgeted suspiciously. Looking closer, I saw he'd purposefully covered his hands in mud and had them hidden—he thought—behind his back, ready to hold them up in front of my face when it was his turn for inspection.

"Adolpho!" I smiled and shook my finger at him.

He roared with laughter and pointed at me—so different from the kid who'd dropped to the ground in abject terror at the slightest contact.

The volunteers and children recited the Lord's Prayer in Spanish before every meal.

> *Padre nuestro*
> *que estás en el cielo,*
> *santificado sea tu nombre.*
> *Venga tu reino . . .*

For the kids, the rituals of the church and the rituals of the home provided a steady, true ground in a life that had been racked by wave after wave of false promises and false starts.

I grew up in St. Louis, Missouri, and had two younger brothers.

With my brothers and cousins after a high school soccer game.

The shifu smashing bricks over the heads of kung fu students in a test of their strength and willpower.

In Croatia, I worked with refugee children who had lost their homes.

I heard many horrible stories of what refugees lived through.
I wondered what this girl's experience had been.

One of the teenagers set up a soccer team for some of the youngest kids. I served as a coach.

In the refugee camps in Zaire, I saw that many young children had to take care of one another.

The genocide in Rwanda was horrific. This is what I saw inside a church. People would seek shelter in churches from bands of thugs, but even there they weren't safe.

The people of Rwanda never gave up hope, and when I took photographs I was often welcomed with smiles.

At the Mano Amiga home in Bolivia, children of the street were cared for by adults and, in turn, learned to care for one another.

Juan Carlos, one of the children of the street, died as a result of poor medical care.

Many street children in Bolivia hold white bottles of "glue" to their noses. Sniffing this cheap drug eases pain and eventually leads to permanent brain damage.

I learned a lot about life from my boxing coaches. They taught me about courage, both in and out of the ring.

I had a great time studying abroad at Oxford University, but even after years of graduate school, I still couldn't put on my tie straight.

At Basic Underwater Demolition/SEAL (BUD/S) training, we would often endure "surf torture" and lie in freezing cold water.

BUD/S classes start with more than two hundred students. By the end, only a few dozen remain.

These men are running off of the infamous grinder, where trainees crank out thousands of pushups and sit-ups.

Running on the soft sand in boots was brutal,
but the scenery was often gorgeous.

As each day passed,
the line of helmets
grew longer as more
men rang out.

Drown-proofing is one of BUD/S's most feared evolutions. Before one swim test, our feet were bound to prevent us from kicking and our hands were tied behind our back. After swimming fifty yards, we had to retrieve a face mask from the bottom of the pool.

Log PT is a particularly painful evolution, meant to test teamwork as much as endurance. The logs weigh more than one hundred pounds and get slippery when covered with sand and water.

During rock portage, worry began to set in. We could control a lot of things—how we worked as a team, whether to quit or to endure. But none of us could control a fierce wave, a tossed boat.

Every day presented new challenges. I tried to stay focused on the task at hand and not dwell on people quitting or leaving because of injury.

Pure exhaustion sometimes caused us to fall asleep at weird times, even during meals.

In the demo pit, students practice taking cover during incoming artillery fire. Practice creates habit; I fell into this position when my team was hit by a suicide truck bomb in Iraq.

Let the games begin—it's the beginning of Hell Week.

Here I am with James Suh during a training evolution in the California desert. James was one of the smartest guys in our class, and he helped others pass dive physics. He became a good friend of mine. Suh died in Afghanistan, when he flew in to rescue another one of our friends, Matt Axelson.

Standing with the commanding officer on the day of my graduation from BUD/S.

In Fallujah, Iraq. After finishing BUD/S training, I served overseas.

Though I didn't have a very structured religious upbring-
ing—my mom is Jewish, my dad Catholic, so we celebrated
a bit of everything—I could see why it mattered to the kids.
They needed something solid and constant, because the streets
always tugged at them.

LOST BOY

Jason suggested I take some of the kids to the soccer stadium in Santa Cruz to watch a game. When I mentioned the outing to a group of older boys, they started shouting and jumping around the room.

"Yes, Quí Qué, yes!"

"Quí Qué is the best, the best, the best!"

How could I resist?

As we left the home the night of the game, the kids had a bounce to their step. Pablo whistled at a girl. Rodrigo spiraled around us and let out an open-throated cheer for his team.

"Rodrigo, please, calm down."

"Yes, Quí Qué, okay. Hey, Quí Qué, give me the money for the *micro,* and I will pay." He looked at me theatrically, eyes pleading. I handed him the money, and he stuffed it into the pocket of his red jacket and yelled, "Thanks, Quí Qué!" and took two fast steps, pretending to run off with the money.

Now that we were out of the home and on the kids' turf, they were full of advice.

"Make sure you put your wallet in your front pocket. You don't want it to get stolen."

"And be careful when stepping into the *micro*."

"Yeah, and if you stand right at this exact spot, you can jump on and get a good seat. You don't want to get run over. Stand back and watch me, Quí Qué."

The *micro*, a boxy little van teeming with people, pulled up through the dust.

A kid hung out the door and shouted, "To the Centro!"

Passengers stepped off, clutching small children and plastic bags filled with groceries.

I piled in after the boys, and we crowded onto the seats.

"Here we go, Quí Qué!"

We raced through the heart of the city, past beautiful stately houses encircled by towering concrete walls. Jagged glass from beer bottles topped the walls to prevent the unwanted — like the kids traveling with me — from climbing over.

We flew past little stands selling tortillas, past bakeries, past hair salons. We crossed a bridge over a canal that carried away the sewage of the city, and we saw a family picking through garbage in the runoff.

"Quí Qué, look," said one of the boys, pointing down an alley. "That's where I used to live."

The energy of the boys boiled over, and when we stepped out of the *micro*, they bolted for the stadium.

"Hey!" I yelled after them.

They turned back.

"Let's be . . ." I searched for a Spanish word for "cool," but nothing came, so I settled on "calm."

"Hey, Quí Qué, buy us seats, buy us seats!"

We already had tickets, but the boys wanted me to buy the

cushions for sale at the entrance—plastic shopping bags full of shredded newspaper.

"Why?"

"Come on, Quí Qué."

"Quí Qué, we need them to sit on."

"We already have tickets."

"But it's good for your—" They laughed as they used a word for "butt" that I'd never heard.

"Come on, let's go in."

The boys punched and wrestled each other, shoving wildly as I hustled them into the stadium, a giant concrete oval with concrete steps for seats. Now I understood why the guy selling the makeshift cushions had so many customers. The kids thought I was a tightwad for not buying them.

"Nice seats, Quí Qué," Pablo said. "Now my butt hurts."

But we didn't sit for long. As soon as the game started, the stadium exploded with energy. The boys yelled and carried on, and all around us men stomped their feet, drummed, sang, and shouted.

The tickets we'd bought were cheap even by Bolivian standards. We stood next to shirtless men covered in dust, clearly having come to the stadium after a day of hard labor. Some of them tore open the newspaper cushions and lit them on fire, adding more and more newspapers until the fire grew and the crowd drew back.

A fire burned in the stands, and the players kept playing. The ref kept making calls. The fans kept shouting.

This is crazy, I thought. *This is great.* I jumped with the kids and shouted, *"¡Vamos!"* I didn't even know the name of the team we were cheering for.

The other team scored goal after goal against ours, and when our side seemed unable to press back on offense, the crowd grew restless. Someone fired what looked like a bottle rocket at the opposing goalkeeper, and it exploded in the grass. I can't remember if they sold beer or if the men smuggled it in, but when the game ended and we left in a tight throng, I was struck by the smell of sweat and cheap alcohol. It had grown dark, and the air held the electric energy of men looking to fight.

With the day's fun over, I drew a relieved breath when we finally stepped out of the stadium.

"Okay," I told the boys. "Head count."

One, two, three, four, five, six . . .

Oh no. I'd come with seven.

I did it again. *One, two, three, four, five, six . . .*

I looked the boys over as, now exhausted, they shuffled from foot to foot.

Who was missing?

Rodrigo.

"Where's Rodrigo?"

"He was just here," one of the boys said.

"Okay. Let's wait for him."

Fans flowed out of the stadium, and I scanned the crowd. Maybe he'd been separated from us in the crush. He'd show up any minute.

Slowly, the crowds dwindled. When a single drunken man stumbled out, I realized I'd lost Rodrigo.

I couldn't return to Mano Amiga minus one child. And what would happen to him? Then I remembered something that Rodrigo had told me: he'd once collected fares on the *micros*. He knew the whole city and many of the drivers. He wasn't lost, I realized; he was off on a little adventure.

Unfortunately, that meant he could be anywhere. The streets, Jason and Caroline told me, pulled constantly at many of the children, especially those who'd experienced the pain and pleasure-filled freedom of sex and drugs, violence and drifting.

"Where is Rodrigo?" I asked the boys again.

"We were just following you. We don't know," they said.

They were unable to suppress their smiles, and it took a measured effort for me to remain calm. They understood our situation perfectly. Rodrigo's disappearance had created an adventure for them all.

"Okay. Follow me," I said, hoping a plan would materialize as I walked. I headed in the direction of the *micro* stands, unsure what I'd do when we arrived.

The kids bounced behind me. I thought, *Should I talk to the police? Should I wait in one spot?*

At one point, I realized that in my nervousness, I'd outpaced them. I turned and did another quick count: *One, two, three, four, five . . . Five heads! I lost another kid.*

Frustrated, I scanned the street. Carlos had fallen behind, chatting with a girl.

"Carlos, come on."

"Quí Qué, I'll catch up soon."

"Carlos!"

"Yes, Quí Qué," he said, as he jogged to rejoin our pack.

As we wandered down the streets, the kids drifted away just far enough to linger outside shops, to yell to girls. We walked down street after street for hours.

"Quí Qué, let's do this every night!"

I sighed. I couldn't stay out all night, but I also couldn't return to the home one kid short. I kept turning corners, hoping to spot Rodrigo.

Then it dawned on me what I should have done from the beginning. I gathered the boys. "Okay, if we find Rodrigo in the next thirty minutes, I'll take you all out tomorrow night to get ice cream."

"This way, Quí Qué, this way!" The kids ran, and I took off after them down an alley, into a square, and past three policemen who—seeing a white guy chasing Bolivian children—started to follow.

"It's good, it's good," I called back to them. "No problem."

"There he is!" one of the boys shouted, and we all stopped running.

I spotted Rodrigo's red jacket and the back of his head where he stood in a line at a *micro* stand.

"Okay. Be quiet, all of you."

I walked up behind Rodrigo, grabbed him by his shoulders, and turned him to me. It didn't hit me until that moment how worried I'd been.

"Where were you? What were you doing?"

He rattled off a response that I couldn't understand, but a lying fourteen-year-old in Bolivia is the same as a lying fourteen-year-old in America and I understood him well enough. I grabbed a fistful of his jacket and propelled him toward the *micro*. The other kids formed a circle around us: close enough to laugh at Rodrigo but not too close to me. We hopped on a *micro* and made our way back to Mano Amiga.

"Thanks, Quí Qué!" the boys yelled as they ran into the home.

I watched Rodrigo go, wondering about him, about whether he or any of the others would ultimately give in to the streets.

JUAN CARLOS

Even though we tried to keep the boys safe and healthy, it sometimes felt like a battle that could never really be won. One day Juan Carlos, a boy from Don Bosco—a neighboring home for children of the street—was taken to the hospital. His injuries were minor—a broken collarbone—and he was expected to recover quickly, but poor medical care caused complications that led to an infection. Soon he contracted typhoid and died.

They brought his body to a small chapel near the home, and some of the boys went to see him. When Eddie and Adolpho walked in, they approached the open casket hesitantly. It rested on a pedestal three or four feet high, and I had to hoist Adolpho up and hold him so he could see his friend.

Juan Carlos lay at peace, his face smooth and even younger-looking in death. Dark hair, neatly combed. Closed eyes. He wore a crisp white shirt and clean navy pants. A plastic cross rested against his narrow chest.

The boys said a prayer and ran out. Part of me wanted to

go with them, back out into the sunshine, to a place full of life. But I sat there, keeping vigil, as other boys came in to pay their respects.

Fourteen-year-old Pablo walked in with Carlos, ten. They stood side by side looking at the body. Then Pablo laid his arm over Carlos's shoulder, in direct imitation, I thought, of Jason when he comforted the boys.

Eddie came to me at lunch and dove onto my legs. I pulled him up.

"*¿Cómo estás,* Eddie?"

"*Bien.*"

But he wasn't. He lay down, and I held him as if he were a baby, his head resting in the crook of my elbow, his eyes shut, his limbs still. For a child normally so energetic, it was odd. No punching, no singing, no monster faces.

In Spanish he said, "I am like Juan Carlos." He folded his hands in prayer over his chest.

"Do you think that Juan Carlos is asleep?" I asked, careful in my Spanish.

"No, he's dead."

"Do you think that Juan Carlos is in heaven?"

"No, he's in the chapel."

At the Mass for Juan Carlos, I stood against the wall, my camera in my hands. I wanted to share this; I wanted people to know what had happened here. All the statistics about poverty and health care in the Third World meant nothing to most people. Viewing just a single picture of this boy, who died because of a broken bone, might make people understand. But this was a Mass, and it didn't feel right to shoot pictures, so I kept my camera at my side.

I learned that Juan Carlos's mother was dead, but his father appeared in the chapel that day. He had wet, red eyes and a slight, birdlike body. For his son's funeral, he wore a brown jacket and pants with Converse sneakers.

I watched him and asked myself why, if Juan Carlos had a father, had he ended up in a home for street children? Was his father abusive? Had he loved his son? Dumped him in the streets? I wanted to understand, but it all seemed so pointless. It made no sense to me.

A priest hurried into the church, almost half an hour late. In view of the congregation, he slipped a robe on over a nylon sweatsuit wet from the day's rain. He spoke of his experience with funerals of children and the admirable way that the community had dealt with this death. He mentioned Juan Carlos's name just twice, filling his talk with stock platitudes.

I hadn't known the boy, but I could imagine how little comfort those who loved him drew from the generic service. Did no one care? He wasn't my brother, my son, or my friend, and I still felt angry at this cursory treatment.

I'd heard that Juan Carlos's injury resulted from his slipping in the shower at Don Bosco. I'd also heard that they'd invented this story so the hospital would admit the boy, though I didn't understand why a lie was necessary. The other story was that Juan Carlos—who had been in and out of the home for most of his life—had been brought to Don Bosco and left there, broken bone and all, by his father.

• • •

A steady rain turned the roads muddy as we drove from the church to the cemetery. They'd loaded Juan Carlos's coffin into the back of a pickup truck, and it jutted over the edge, resting haphazardly on the open gate. I had nightmare visions of the coffin sliding free, tumbling into the road, but a group of older boys from Don Bosco climbed into the back. They clung to the coffin as we bounced over rough roads and potholes. Each time the truck hit a bump in the road, the boys tightened their grip. We kept our windows open, and I listened to the slap of rain on metal and wood, the roar of the engine, and the splatter of the mud.

At the paupers' cemetery where the dead were interred in walled crypts, I once again felt the urge to take pictures. I wanted the world to honor Juan Carlos and for people to ask themselves what they could do for boys like him.

I found a woman who seemed to be a relative and asked her permission.

"Yes, please," she said, squeezing my arm for emphasis. "I want you to share this with people."

I moved to the back of the crowd and raised my camera.

The same priest who'd led the lackluster church service spoke at the burial site. In conclusion, he intoned, *"Adiós, hijo"*(Goodbye, son). Or was it *"A Dios, hijo"* (To God, son)?

Silent until that moment, the dead boy's father threw back his head and wailed, as if he'd only just then realized that his son was truly dead. He touched the casket, and his fingers lingered there. His shoulders shook with violent sobs as he finally released his son to his final resting place.

The older boys lifted the coffin to their shoulders and slid it into its slot. A bricklayer dressed in speckled pants walked over and quickly, cleanly, set the bricks and applied the mortar, sealing Juan Carlos in with the other lost children of the street.

When almost everyone else had left, a young woman wrote, with her index finger, an epitaph in the still-wet mortar:

J. CO. R.

eres un angelito

que

estás en cielo

Juan Carlos

you are a little angel

who

is in heaven

Back at Mano Amiga, Eddie found me to play a game. He told me, "Juan Carlos is not in the chapel now."

A NEW PERSPECTIVE

In my senior year at Duke, I applied for a Rhodes Scholarship, which would provide full tuition and a small stipend to study at Oxford University in England. Awarded to just thirty-two American men and women each year, the scholarship is granted to candidates for "character, commitment to others and to the common good, and for their potential for leadership in whatever domains their careers may lead."[8]

A tall order, but I had high hopes. Doing humanitarian work overseas, I realized it isn't enough to fight for a better world; we also have to live lives worth fighting *for*. I thought Oxford might help me in that pursuit.

The Rhodes committee granted the scholarship, and for the next four years, I attended graduate school in England. There I really began to appreciate how beautiful life could be. I fell in love, boxed for Oxford's championship team, attended all-night dinner parties, went on a study trip in the French Alps, walked cobbled paths with friends while we debated ideas, and learned as much from the diverse population of students as I did from my excellent professors.

Amid the pleasures of Oxford life, I still felt determined to find a pathway for effective humanitarian work. I even wrote a dissertation on the topic with a simple thesis: What matters for the long-term health and vitality of people who have suffered is not what they are given, but what they *do*. Rather than choosing for them and making them passive recipients of goodwill, it was better to empower them to make their own choices. And rather than simply giving aid to children, it made sense to support children, families, and communities that were already engaged in their own recovery.

Along the way, I became an advocate for using power, where necessary, to protect the weak, to halt ethnic cleansing, to end genocide. But when I was writing papers and speaking at conferences to make this argument, my words seemed hollow. I was really saying (in so many words) that *someone else* should go do the dangerous work that I thought was so important. How could I ask others to put themselves in harm's way if I hadn't done so myself?

When I was a kid, if you'd asked me what I wanted to be when I grew up, it's unlikely that I would have said "soldier" or "sailor." Like most boys, my brothers and I pretended to shoot each other with Wiffle Ball bats, and we lobbed plastic bowling pins as pretend grenades. But I had no more interest in the military than I did in dinosaurs or outer space.

When I remembered kids in Croatia drawing chalk pictures of the homes they'd been forced to flee at gunpoint, or when I thought about standing at the open door of a church in Rwanda and staring at piles of skeletal remains, it became more and more clear to me that all of the protests, articles, and policy papers in the world had their limits. It took people with courage to protect those in need of protection. I could keep talking, or I could live my beliefs.

So, between reading articles about land mine–clearing projects in Afghanistan and microfinance programs in Bangladesh, I researched the U.S. Navy's Sea, Air, and Land (SEAL) teams.

The U.S. Navy offered the most direct route into special operations, and the SEALs were famous for having the toughest military training in the world. I thought: if I'm going to do this—join the military—why not really test myself?

As a SEAL, I'd not only have the chance to jump out of airplanes, scuba-dive, and drive fast boats, but also, at a deeper level, I'd be offered an opportunity to lead and the chance to serve my country. By the time I finished my dissertation, I was twenty-six. The cutoff age for the SEAL teams was twenty-eight.

It was now or never.

I took the bus to London to meet two SEALs working there. At the time, I had an offer to stay at Oxford and begin an academic career. I also had an offer to join a consulting firm, where I would have earned more money in my first twelve months of work than my parents had ever earned in a year combined. I thought about all of the freedom that Oxford promised. I thought about all the wealth that the consulting firm offered me. And then I listened to the deal that the United States Navy put on the table.

If my application was accepted—"And we'll accept fewer than ten this year," they told me—they'd send me to Officer Candidate School. The Navy would pay me $1,332.60 per month. I would submit to the Navy's rules and regulations, and in my first months in the military, I would have zero minutes per day of privacy.

If I graduated from Officer Candidate School, the Navy would make me an officer, but in turn I would owe them eight years of service. They would offer me one and only one chance to pass Basic Underwater Demolition/SEAL (BUD/S) training. If I passed, I'd be on my way to becoming a SEAL officer and leader. If I failed, as over 80 percent of the men who entered SEAL training did, I would still owe the Navy eight years, and they would tell me where and how I would serve.

Contemplating the different paths before me, I thought about the rotunda of the Rhodes House mansion at Oxford, whose walls are etched with the names of Rhodes Scholars who died during the two world wars. Seeing those names reminded me that the scholarship was intended to help create public servants who would "fight the world's fight."

Oxford could give me time. The consulting firm could give me money. The SEAL teams would give me little, but make me more. I thought, *I might fail at BUD/S, I might be miserable, but I'll live with no regrets.*

I signed the papers as soon as they put them in front of me.

NOT IN OXFORD ANYMORE

I landed in Pensacola, Florida, on January 20, 2001, for Officer Candidate School (OCS), and immediately I had doubts. I wanted to serve my country. I wanted to be tested. The strong often need to protect the weak, and I believed that rather than talking about what should be done, I should do it. At the same time, I was leaving a life of extraordinary freedom that I absolutely enjoyed and felt reluctant to sacrifice.

At Oxford, I had done pretty much as I pleased. I'd spent whole days reading novels — *The Grapes of Wrath, The Color Purple* — in the University Parks. When I wanted to serve at one of Mother Teresa's homes for the destitute and dying, I went to India. I trained nine times a week with the boxing team, but every time I showed up, I did so by choice. I had days, weeks, months, years at my disposal. At Oxford, I learned and trained, lived and served, on my own schedule.

At OCS, I knew I'd be lucky to steal two minutes to myself. I'd read that they made candidates fight two to a sink to shave in just minutes. My material possessions had always been minimal — bed, books, boxing gear — but I'd always lived in comfortable places with time on my hands.

I was entering a world where they issued every candidate a thick rule book to study, memorize, and obey. The rule book was to be placed on the desk such that the right side of the book ran parallel to the right side of the desk exactly one-half inch from the edge, and the bottom of the book ran parallel to the bottom of the desk exactly one-half inch from the edge.

In the U.S. Navy, they had rules about rules.

My concern that I'd made a mistake deepened during my first few days at OCS. Once on base, I was greeted by candidate officers—those in the final two weeks of the thirteen-week program who were put in charge of the incoming candidates. One of these guys—sweating, slightly pudgy, his head shaved—yelled at me to "Walk faster!" as his face broke out in red blotches.

Is he kidding?

I lined up on a sidewalk with the other recruits. I wore jeans, hiking boots, and the same faded safari shirt I'd worn to China eight years earlier. As I dropped my red duffel bag at my feet, I thought about the things I'd seen since then, the people who had inspired me. And for the hundredth time in just a few hours, I asked myself whether I'd chosen the right path.

One candidate officer was sweating, and the cracked timbre of his voice gave away his nervousness. "You want to be a Navy officer?!" he yelled.

No, I thought. *I'm here for the buffet.*

They marched us around the base in our civilian clothes, yelling at us to stand straight, take our hands out of our pockets. It seemed they had only one volume—loud—and it felt over-the-top and immature to me. Earl Blair had demanded extraordinary performance, but I had never once heard him yell at or berate one of his fighters. In Bolivia, Jason and Caroline had presided over dozens of unruly and often troubled children without screaming commands.

"Drink water! Drink more water! Every fountain you pass, you will stop and drink water!"

I had boxed for years. I knew exactly how much water I needed to drink.

A candidate officer shadowed us. "Do what you're told, and you'll have nothing to fear!"

I must not have looked sufficiently panicked, because a candidate officer got in my face. "Just wait until your drill instructor shows up," he threatened. "You'll be doing pushups until your arms fall off!"

I allowed myself the small rebellion of cocking an eyebrow at him.

The candidate officers had been in the Navy exactly eleven weeks longer than I had, and most of them were younger by a few years. Thanks to Hollywood, I'd expected to be greeted by tough drill sergeants, hard-driving veterans who would push exhausted recruits to their limits. That would have been a test. I looked forward to being pushed by people who had served and earned the right to train me. These guys, strutting around in their recently issued black Navy windbreakers, just seemed like jerks. As they walked up and down the rows of recruits, I wondered, *Is this the kind of leadership the military produces? All yelling and ego?*

Some of my fellow classmates were so intimidated that their hands shook when they bent to tie their shoes. Now dressed in a set of ill-fitting plain green fatigues, I sat down to eat in the chow hall across from another candidate. The yelling had gotten to him, and after forcing down water all day, he promptly puked a full canteen's worth of bile across the table, soaking me.

Yep, Eric. You're not in Oxford anymore.

After chow they ran us back to the barracks and made us stand in the hallway. Finally, our drill instructor Staff Sergeant Lewis appeared—a comic-book-like figure of Marine Corps perfection striding down the corridor, his face hidden beneath his Smokey Bear hat, his biceps emerging from his perfectly rolled sleeves, boots shining, baritone booming. "Get out of my passageway! Stand against the bulkhead!"

I watched with anthropologist-like fascination. *I wonder if the drill instructors practice this,* I thought, *the walking-down-the-hallway moment.*

Staff Sergeant Lewis grabbed me by the collar of my fatigues, shoved me against the wall, and yelled, "Join the rest of this sorry group!"

It struck me then: I was actually in the Navy.

He yelled at us to run around the barracks, and in her panic, one woman ran in the wrong direction down the hallway. Staff Sergeant Lewis flew into a rage.

"Get over here now!" he screamed. He grabbed her by her lapels and threw her down the passageway.

After hearing a command, we were to told to yell "Kill!" and then execute the command.

"Eyes right!"

"Kill!"

"Forward, march!"

"Kill!"

I looked across the hallway to see if any of the other candidates found this as ridiculous as I did. Only one of them rolled his eyes back at me.

"Kill!"

I doubted this group of largely untested and almost uniformly out-of-shape college grads could kill time, let alone a dangerous foe.

"Your name is on your room. Get there!"

I ran to find my room, which I shared with three other recruits, and once clear of the candidate officers and the drill instructor, I sat down and started to laugh. My roommates watched me, wide-eyed with fear, and I imagined their thoughts: *Oh no, the pressure's gotten to this guy—he's cracking already.*

IRONING UNDERWEAR

The next few days did nothing for my confidence in my decision. They issued us workout clothes that were as dysfunctional—swim trunks with no drawstring—as they were unfashionable, and I began to learn some basic Navy lingo. A door was a "hatch," a wall was a "bulkhead," a bathroom was a "head." Women were not women but "females." To say something was to "put the word out." To be quiet was to "lock it up."

Teams of drill instructors swarmed as we ate meals of overcooked food. They strode along tabletops, using their boots to kick silverware and glasses onto the floor. If they spotted a candidate committing some minor infraction, they'd knock the tray out of his hands and send spaghetti flying through the air.

They also focused obsessively on clothes. We spent hours folding our shirts and shorts and pants. We actually sprayed starch—a lot of it—on our underwear, ironed it into perfect squares, and then stacked those flat squares in our lockers for inspection. We received two pairs of running shoes, but the word came down to avoid wearing one pair so they'd always be clean for inspection. It all seemed absurd.

I expected runs so fast my lungs would burn. Instead, we ran in formation as a class. In my training, I'd run six-minute miles. Now I shuffled through twelve-minute miles while singing silly songs.

> Mission top secret, destination unknown
> We don't know if we're ever coming home
> Stand up, buckle up, and shuffle to the door . . .

I actually felt my physical conditioning slipping away. When were we going to train hard? Was this really my life? I'd joined the Navy for a challenge, yet at night we spent time cutting loose strings—"Irish pennants"—from our uniforms and then dabbing the spots with fingernail polish to keep the strays from returning.

This is my challenge? Fingernail polish?

I worried about dealing with eight years of this. Eight years of slow-motion "running." Eight years of thread snipping. Eight years of folding underwear stiff enough to make into paper airplanes.

Where was the test in all of this? How was I supposed to serve?

STEPPING UP

One morning during physical training, we were doing push-ups when a drill instructor began screaming at a member of our class. "What are you doing to my gym floor, candidate?"

Wong — a slight man with ambitions of becoming a civil engineer in the U.S. Navy — had been instructed, as we all had, to keep a straight back during pushups. But Wong couldn't do it. His back sagged so that his crotch brushed the ground.

"What are you doing?!" the instructor screamed again. "You are defiling my gym floor! Are you lonely here?!"

Wong swiveled his hips in an attempt to straighten his back.

"Oh my goodness! That is one of the most disgusting frickin' acts of violence against a piece of United States Navy property that I have ever seen!"

Staff Sergeant Lewis strode over to Wong, looming over him with fury. "What is the matter with you, Wong?" he hollered. And then he looked around and called, "Where is that Gritchens?"

I looked around at the others, but no one stepped forward. Realization dawned.

Did he mean me?

"Gritchens, get over here!"

I jumped up and ran over to Staff Sergeant Lewis.

"Yes, sir!"

"Gritchens, Wong here just became your personal project—do you understand me?"

"Yes, sir!"

"You are going to teach Wong how to do pushups! You are going to move into the same room as Wong, wake at the same time as Wong, and you will teach Wong in every spare moment so that Wong *will* pass the final physical fitness test. I am going to hold you responsible for Wong's PT." He closed the space between us, and I felt his eyes drilling into me. "Do you understand?"

"Yes, sir!"

He walked away, and for a moment I felt resentful of the responsibility I'd been given. But then I got it.

I had to make my peace with OCS. I wanted to serve, and I couldn't change the school. I couldn't make us actually run instead of jog and sing. I couldn't change the curriculum so that we learned how to fire shotguns instead of polishing belt buckles. None of that was in my control.

I'd imagined that OCS would turn me into a leader through difficult physical tests like obstacle courses, runs, and rescue swims, or through hard classroom learning and precision military maneuvers—learning how to march, to drill with a rifle, to shoot a pistol. I was wrong on all counts, but now I realized I had an opportunity here. I had the chance to lead others, to be of genuine help to my classmates. OCS would be easy for me, but for some of the men and women in my class, it was the test of their lives. If I had joined the military to be of service, here was my chance.

I threw myself into the regimen. I moved in with Wong as ordered. We'd take breaks every ten minutes while working on our uniforms to knock out fifteen or twenty pushups. He got stronger.

I became the "PT Body," the person in charge of the physical training of the class. My friend Matt and I organized the dramatically named "Deathwish PT," and in the evening we'd take a group from our class outside for extra physical training. No one came close to death, but we did have a lot of fun. We'd knock out pull-ups and blow off steam by laughing about the day. Wong in particular impressed me. He must have known OCS would be hard on him, but he'd still signed up.

OCS offered recognition — in the form of a white badge called a snowflake — to any man or woman who graduated with excellence in all three areas of endeavor: physical training, academic tests, and military proficiency. We worked together as a class and made it our goal to graduate with more snowflakes than any other class in our year. We started to cooperate in small ways. I was, for example, never very good at shining shoes, so I made deals with classmates: I washed their sneakers, and they polished my shoes. Our class was given a "guide-on," a flag, and we marched with it everywhere we went.

The school remained disappointing. In class the instructors would issue a statement and stomp their feet on the floor.

"Buoys are considered an aid to navigation." *Stomp. Stomp.*

"What's with that?" I asked a classmate on the first day.

"That means that'll be a question on the test," came the response.

"Why don't they just say, 'This is going to be on the test'?"

"'Cause they're not allowed to tell us what's on the test."

Often we stayed up late preparing our uniforms and fell asleep in classes the next day. We continued to polish belt buckles and snip threads. Almost all of us slept in sleeping bags *on* our beds rather than *in* them because we didn't want to have to take twenty minutes in the morning to prepare our beds again for inspection.

One night we had a mishap. Wong, like some of the other guys, used a cigarette lighter instead of scissors to rid his uniform of Irish pennants. The night before an inspection, Wong's technique failed, and he burned a three-finger-sized hole in one of his khaki uniform shirts.

On the morning of the inspection, the drill instructors discovered Wong's shirt and exploded.

"Wong, drop down!"

With Wong in pushup position, they pulled every item out of his locker—starched underwear, starched socks, laundry bag, knit cap, pants, belt buckles—and threw them onto the floor.

"What is the matter with you people?" one of the instructors yelled. "How are you going to let Wong over here *burn holes* in his uniform? What did you think was going to happen when we walked in here?!"

We had no response.

The drill instructor continued. "Oh, Wong, your uniform looks great except for this *fist-sized hole* that you burned straight through your shirt."

We stood at attention, and I bit the inside of my mouth, trying not to laugh.

"How do you expect to stand in front of your sailors as an officer, as a leader, when you do not have common sense enough to not burn holes in your uniform!"

Staff Sergeant Lewis walked into the room, which now looked like it had been hit by a hurricane. He sized up the situation and gave me a fierce look. "Gritchens! What is going on here?"

Another drill instructor answered for me. "Wong here has gotten all creative, a 100 percent individual, and I think Gritchens enrolled him in a goddarn contemporary frickin' fashion class!" He held up the burned uniform. "That is some avant-garde frickin' runway-model trash right here!"

Staff Sergeant Lewis boomed, "Gritchens, I told you to watch out for Wong! What is going on?!"

"No excuse, sir!" I said. "It's my responsibility, sir!"

One of the drill instructors asked, "Wong, have you ever played a goddarn sport in your life?!"

Wong surprised them by yelling up from the floor, "Yes, sir!"

"Really?" the drill instructor asked. "What sport did you play?"

"Football, sir!"

The drill instructors looked at each other in disbelief. "Really, Wong, you played football? What position did you play?"

Wong yelled, "It was John Madden Football, sir!"

One of the drill instructors walked out of the room in an effort to control a laugh. The other drill instructor bent down close to Wong's ear and yelled, "Computer games are not a sport! Do you understand me?!"

Staff Sergeant Lewis ordered the other two men out of the room to join the class at chow.

I prepared for an onslaught of abuse, but for the first time Staff Sergeant Lewis addressed me like a human being—albeit a gruff human being. "Gritchens, Wong is going to miss breakfast. I want you to run down to the McDonald's and buy him something to eat."

"Yes, sir!"

From where we stood in the passageway, Staff Sergeant Lewis couldn't see Wong, but I could. He yelled, "Wong, Gritchens is going to McDonald's to get you breakfast—what do you want?"

From my vantage point, I saw the drill instructor bend down near Wong's ear and whisper, "You better tell him, 'Lewis, go get me a goddarn frickin' Egg McMuffin.' Say exactly that, or I will beat you for days."

Wong yelled, "Lewis, go get me a god—n f—kin' Egg McMuffin!"

Staff Sergeant Lewis exploded into the room and, with the other drill instructor, worked Wong through a series of pushups and squat thrusts until he'd created a huge pool of sweat on the ground.

HOW IT'S DONE

We marched as a class, trained as a class, studied as a class. We passed inspections, and we passed exams. We managed, eventually, to get in and out of the chow hall without having trays knocked out of our hands.

I also started to have a good time. We earned the freedom of our Saturdays, and we'd all head out—dressed in our goofy candidate uniforms—and laugh for hours over plates of hot wings and burgers. I got to know my fellow candidates better, and I liked them even more. They'd all come to serve.

While driving off base with my friends one day, I realized that if I counted the years from the time I became an adult at age eighteen to the time I joined the military at nearly twenty-seven, I'd spent more time outside the United States than I'd spent in it.

I'd learned a lot about the world, but now, back at home, I was being reintroduced to America by some of our best people, those who had dedicated themselves to serving our country.

We wore the same uniforms, had the same haircuts, and spoke the same military language—but we retained a rich diversity of thought, humor, and philosophy. My fellow officer candidates were—almost to a person—kind and thoughtful, and it was through them that I began to rediscover America.

We helped each other in many ways. When one man's mother became very ill, and he broke down crying at the thought of leaving the Navy to return home, I listened and tried to counsel him. When another friend fell apart seven weeks into OCS and thought he wanted to quit, I talked him into staying. He'd just never believed in himself before, and I did what I could to make him feel worthy.

Even though I still found the underwear folding and thread snipping ridiculous, I began to see the wisdom of our training. All of the yelling and all of the tests were meant to prepare us for what we might experience as ship commanders. These tests didn't come close, I was sure, to reacting to an incoming missile or a sinking ship, but it did begin to teach us that we could, that we had to, manage our fear and perform while under stress.

I'd learned in boxing and in my work overseas that human beings can overcome fear. When I first stepped into a boxing ring to spar, my heart raced, my adrenaline pumped, my muscles were tense—and I got beat up. After years of Earl's training, I could get in a ring with an appreciation of how dangerous my opponent was, but I could keep my heart rate steady, my muscles loose, and I could fight well. The same thing happened as I became more comfortable working in dangerous situations overseas. I didn't dismiss the dangers, but I was able to operate in those places without my fear getting the best of me.

Likewise, while I found the unrelenting inspections of our

uniforms to be mind numbing, it did teach us to pay attention to detail. If one man had lint on the back of his coat, we'd all pay. We learned to look out for each other, quite literally. Though I'd always worked with others and respected being part of a community, joining the Navy made me appreciate even more the importance of teamwork.

Even Staff Sergeant Lewis started to take a bit of pride in our class. He would call out, "One-Five" (we were class 15–01), and we would shout back, "Hell yeah!"

When the day of the final physical fitness test arrived, we were required to complete forty-seven pushups in two minutes. Wong dropped down and knocked out more than ninety. He stood, brushed his hands together with a grin, and said, "Guess that's how it's done." We were all proud of each other.

On graduation day — our class now dressed in tight-collared "choker whites," marching in formation and executing sword salutes — we became officers of the United States Navy.

YOU: LEADING IN DANGER

They call it the grinder. It's where they grind you down. A slab of concrete the size of a basketball court and surrounded by two-story walls, it's where you'll be herded and cursed at while guns sound all around you and cold water from a fire hose is blasted in your face.

Being driven into the grinder, tormented and physically punished, is the first act of a very long week. The instructors try to throw you off balance, to flush out the weak and to separate you from your team.

But there's another way. You've thought it over. When the guns start firing, when the yelling begins and the hoses start to spray, you have a choice. You can run out of the tent with your men, run right into the chaos. Or you can tell your team to crawl out under the sides of the tent, gather together, and run past the mayhem. You can ignore the instructors as they yell at you to drop down for pushups, and you can find a spot to hide your team.

It's sneaky, and it has its risks. If they catch you, the punishment you receive will be severe. You'll be marked for retribution all week long.

But if they don't catch you, you'll start the hardest week of the hardest military training in the world on your own terms. You'll be able to rest for just a few minutes. You'll go into the week having made decisions, bucked the system, avoided pain, just a little bit. And that one little act of defiance might be enough to boost your confidence, and that of your crew, for the entire week.

You sleep, and when you wake, it's to the sound of automatic weapons and air-raid sirens.

It's begun.

You fall to the floor, your men beside you. They look at you for your decision. You can rush out the main exit with your crew, run—with the rest of the class—right into the middle of things, or you can take a chance and crawl under the side of the tent.

What do you do?

THERE IS NO *TRY*

I arrived at the Naval Amphibious Base Coronado in San Diego, California, determined to complete the journey that began with my reading by flashlight as a boy.

The odds were against me. Basic Underwater Demolition/SEAL (BUD/S) training is universally recognized as the hardest military training in the world. Lasting a grueling six months, it pushes candidates to their physical and mental limits. Only about 10 percent of BUD/S students graduate with their original class.

When I arrived, I had no idea what to expect. I was wearing my Navy whites—a pristine uniform—and had an absurd concern that I'd be shoved right into the chaos and dirt of an obstacle course. But after I checked in, they told me to come back the next day to pick up my equipment.

Later I'd find out that we had to stencil our names on everything they gave us in BUD/S: every T-shirt, every knife, every piece of gear. The morning after my arrival, they handed me my fins. On them I found the names of men who'd been issued this gear before me.

~~Walker~~

~~Rodriguez~~

Herman

None of them had made it. I took out a stencil kit, crossed out "Herman," and wrote "Greitens." I wondered if, in a few weeks, they'd issue these fins to someone else who'd cross out *my* name.

That day I sat with Warrant Officer Green on a bench outside his office looking out at the grinder.

"BUD/S is hard for everybody," he told me. "But we're going to make it even harder on you and harder on all the other officers. Everyone will be looking to you for leadership. We expect you to be at the front of the runs, the front of the swims. We expect you to be an example and to set the standard."

I stood up from the bench and shook Warrant Green's hand. As I jogged to the barracks, a hundred worries ran through my mind. They were going to make it even harder on me? How? Was there anything I could do to prepare?

At five a.m. on the first full day of BUD/S, we gathered on the beach. Under any other circumstances, it would have been a morning to enjoy. Waves crashed on the shore and rolled up the sand. Stars shone over the ocean.

This is beautiful, I thought, but I didn't have time to enjoy the scenery.

The instructors walked onto the beach. "Drop!"

We all fell and pressed our hands into the sand. As a class we knocked out pushups in unison.

"Down."

"One!" we boomed.

"Down."

"Two!"

"Down."

"Three!"

An instructor dragged his boot through the sand to make a starting line. He relayed instructions over a bullhorn: "There is a truck parked two miles down the beach. Run down the beach. Run around the truck. Then run back here. You have thirty-two minutes. And, gentlemen . . ." He paused, and then we heard for the first time a line we'd hear thousands of times in BUD/S: "It pays to be a winner."

Headlights cut through the black morning. The truck looked impossibly far away.

"That's not two miles," someone grumbled.

"I heard it's impossible to make it on the first run. Sometimes it's more like five miles."

From the bullhorn came: "Ready." We all took in a breath. "Begin."

In a panic, the pack of men started to sprint. White T-shirts flew past. Men kicked up sand as they ran.

I yelled, "Be steady. Be steady," but fear ruled that morning, and the class flew down the beach. I watched them go, worried that they'd burn themselves out too quickly.

The classmate I ran beside was an accomplished triathlete, and we traded looks of disbelief at the panic around us. As we reached the half-mile mark, the sprinters had slowed desperately, and some were already at a jog. They loped for a bit and then sprinted. They stopped, coughed, and ran again in an erratic rhythm borne of panic. We still had three and a half miles to go, and already these guys were in trouble. These were athletes: high school and college football players, water polo players, state champion wrestlers. Many of them would later ace the runs, but as BUD/S would teach us over and over again, physical fitness mattered little without the mental fortitude to deal with fear.

As we approached the turnaround truck, its headlight beams cut through the morning and lit up a small group of us knotted together near the front of the pack. I ran, half-blinded, into the headlights and heard the instructors yell, "Take off your shirts! Take off your shirts! Throw 'em in the back of the truck!"

The instructors knew every trick. They knew that in the dark, in the confusion of dozens of running men, it would be easy for any one man to make a quick turn on the beach short of the truck and start running back to the finish. Our shirts had our names stenciled on them. They would provide proof that we'd made it to the halfway point.

We peeled off our shirts, tossed them in the back of the truck, and ran for the finish line. Those of us who made it in the designated time were sent to stretch. Those who raced in late were ordered: "Hit the surf! Straight to the water!" The exhausted men went stumbling into the fifty-degree water of the Pacific Ocean.

After a shivering minute, the men dragged themselves, soaking wet, out of the ocean.

"Get sandy!" the instructors yelled, and the men dropped

and rolled until every inch of their bodies was covered in sand.

"Pushups—knock 'em out!" And the men did pushups until they were exhausted, and then they were made to flip over and do flutter kicks. Then it was back to pushups, back to flutter kicks, back to pushups.

"Stand up. Grab a partner. Fireman's-carry drills down the beach. Run to Instructor Wade. Now!" Men on the verge of collapse picked up other soaking two-hundred-pound men and struggled down the beach.

The men ran back into the water, dove in, and then ran back out to the beach. In. Out. In. Out. They did it again and again.

An instructor walked over to those of us stretching and said, "Gentlemen, observe closely. You fail. You pay."

The instructors circled a man who'd failed the run and was now covered in salt water and sand. He was in the pushup position, his arms shaking under the strain of holding himself up.

One instructor yelled at him, "You know what the prize is for second place in a gunfight?"

"Negative, Instructor."

"It's death. There is no prize for second place. Now do your pushups properly."

The man's arms shook and drool hung from his lips as he tried to spit the sand out of his mouth. He must have said something like "I'm trying," because the instructor exploded: "There is no *try*. We do not *try*. Your teammates do not need you to *try* to cover their backs. Your swim buddy does not need you to *try* to rescue him on a dive. Your platoon does not need you to *try* to shoot straight. *There is no* try. *There is only* do."

By the time we ran to breakfast, several men had quit.

The instructors encouraged it. If at any moment in the training a candidate said, "I quit," or, "I D.O.R. [drop on request]," they removed him immediately. Often we never saw him again.

Later the quitters would have to "ring out" by ringing a bell three times. As they left, they'd set their BUD/S helmets on the ground. As each day passed, the line of helmets grew longer. I'd look at those helmets with a kind of relief. Each helmet meant that I had survived, and I was proud to be hanging in there, minute by minute, day by day.

Sometimes they brought the bell out with us while we trained, and you could "express quit" by going straight to the bell.

Each morning I arrived at the base before any hint of the sun. As I pulled in, I often heard hard heavy metal blaring from the barracks. Men dressed in camouflage with shaved heads would mill about the courtyard, trading guesses about what the day might entail.

"Hey, Mr. G."

"What's goin' on, Lipsky?"

"Just another morning in paradise."

I smiled as I walked in to work. If I'd stayed at Oxford to teach or gone to work for that consulting firm, I knew I'd never have gotten up this early or had this much fun. I would have lived my entire life with the same kind of people who went to Duke or Oxford, or who worked at fancy law firms. Almost all of them understood what it meant to be a professor or a lawyer, but few people there understood what it meant to be a police officer or to have a job where you depended on the strength of your back. They thought of themselves as "global citizens," while these men at BUD/S thought of themselves simply as Americans.

GOING DEEP

Much of our BUD/S training took place at the combat training tank, a specially designed Olympic-size pool with sections of varying depths: three feet, nine feet, and fifteen feet.

We ran to the training tank dressed in camouflage shirts, camouflage pants, black boots, and our green "first phase" helmets. Each of us wore a web belt—a thick belt made for carrying gear. Attached to the belt was a canteen, and tied around the top of the canteen was a piece of white rope.

In any free moment—waiting for chow, waiting for our turn to run the obstacle course—we'd practice tying knots. We learned how to tie knots because we needed to be able to attach explosives to obstacles underwater.

The instructors had strung a line in the water in the fifteen-foot section of the tank, just inches from the bottom of the pool. I wasn't the best swimmer in the class, but I knew that if I waited for others to go first, the fear would just build. I needed to set an example, so I jumped into the water with a swim buddy.

We swam to an instructor treading water in front of us. Our

task, he said, was to tie a knot around the rope submerged at the bottom of the pool.

Both of us took a deep breath, made a fist, and pointed our thumbs down to indicate we were about to dive. As we kicked to the bottom of the pool, pressure built on my eardrums. I pinched my nose and blew hard until my ears popped and the pressure equalized.

When we reached the bottom of the pool, I pulled out my rope and started to tie a knot around the line in the water. On dry land it was easy, but underwater I kept floating upward, which meant I had to release the knot to paddle myself down again.

When my swim buddy and I finished tying our knots, we gave the instructor the "Okay?" sign. He exhaled, and a few bubbles ran for the surface. He looked at the left side of our knots, then the right side. He tugged on both knots, and just as I felt I couldn't stay down there much longer, he gave us both the okay. We untied our knots and streaked toward the surface.

Treading water, we took five big breaths. Our instructor said, "Let's go," and we swam down to tie the next knot. We had to do this five times, and each time, it got harder. My fingers grew clumsier. I found it harder to hold my breath.

One of the men in our class swam down and tied his knot. But then he began to float toward the surface, his body limp.

"Everyone out of the pool," they ordered. We climbed out, and they made us sit down, facing away from the casualty. I still heard them drag his body from the water and listened as they worked to revive our classmate. He lived, but he suffered brain damage and left BUD/S.

Lieutenant John Skop, the officer in charge of the BUD/S class two classes before ours, had not been so lucky. He had been doing caterpillar races when it happened. In caterpillar races, teams of men wearing life jackets line up in the pool. Each man wraps his legs around the man in front of him. Connected like an ungainly caterpillar, the men paddle with their arms and race against other teams down the length of the pool.

The instructors warned us over and over again to tell them if we ever coughed up blood, which could be a sign of pulmonary edema. In a pulmonary edema, fluid builds up in the lungs, and it becomes harder and harder to breathe. The lieutenant had kept his pulmonary edema a secret, and when he started to struggle through the caterpillar race, his lungs finally filled with fluid. He died on the pool deck.

When I first heard Skop's story, I thought, *That was stupid. I'd have let the doctors know.* But when I was actually in the middle of BUD/S training, the last thing in the world I wanted to do was to be rolled out of my class for medical reasons and have to start over again with another class of men I didn't know.

In fact, a few weeks later, a friend and fellow member of BUD/S Class 237 caught me spitting out what felt like a lungful of blood after I'd come up from tying a knot at fifty feet.

I said, "I'm fine."

He looked at me and just said, "Come on. Better not let the instructors see you."

For days after, I worried something was wrong, but I kept going.

MR. HALL'S WILD RIDE

As the weeks progressed, our original group of 220 contracted to a smaller class of men we knew, liked, and trusted. Still, even that group grew smaller by the day as people failed or quit.

Men quit as the runs continued and the swims got longer. Men quit in the pool and were hurt on the obstacle course. One man fell forty feet from the high-tower obstacle and broke his legs.

Those who remained dug in and kept going. I tried not to think about those who'd left or been injured. I just tried to take each new day, each new challenge, as it came. We learned how to row our boats as a team and how to make our backpacks float so we could pull them through the ocean at night; we learned how to sharpen our knives and how to patrol as a team.

Many of the evolutions—the tests and challenges—were painful, but one thing we all enjoyed was working with helicopters. The first time we climbed inside one, I had a smile on my face a mile wide. As the rotors started up and the helo lifted free of the ground, I leaned over and yelled to Greg Hall—one of the petty officers in my boat crew—"This is cool!"

He tapped his ear to indicate that he couldn't hear me.

"This is COOOOL!" I yelled.

His face broke into a wide grin, and he gave me a thumbs-up as we flew over San Diego Bay.

The helicopter slowed to ten knots. We flew ten feet above the bay, and the rotors *whomped* and churned the water into a wild froth. I was in charge of a boat crew of seven men, and we all stood and formed a line. When the instructor pointed out the door, the first man jumped. The helo continued to fly, and we jumped at intervals one after another, inserting a long string of swimmers in the water. Hall was the second-to-last man to jump.

A former U.S. Marine and college football player, Greg Hall was a rock. He had a ready sense of humor, but he was also dead serious about getting done whatever job was set in front of him. In a class full of young and inexperienced men, Hall was a beacon of strength and maturity. I'd come to trust him completely.

We were practicing a method of inserting and extracting SEALs during an operation. A helo would fly in and drop off a team in the water. The team would conduct a mission, swim back out into the ocean, and the helicopter would lower a ladder, fly by, and pick up the team.

I was the last man out of the helo. The instructor held his fist in the hold sign, and then he pointed out the door. I jumped, joining the men afloat in the water. The helicopter flew a wide circle around the bay and dropped its ladder as it turned to fly back over us again.

Now the test began. Each man in our boat crew had to grab the ladder as it was dragged through the water and then climb up the ladder and back into the helo.

Hall checked to see that we were all in a straight line, then held his arm high out of the water and gave me a thumbs-up. The helicopter whirred above us. The first man in our crew grabbed the ladder and climbed. He'd made it up three rungs—perfectly done—when the ladder reached the second man.

Yap was a commando from Singapore who had come to BUD/S to train with American special operations forces. As he grabbed for the ladder, it twisted, making it difficult for him to climb up. By the time the ladder reached the third man, Yap was only on the first rung. This left no room for the next man, who grabbed the ladder and was dragged through the water. Still, the helo kept flying, and the men kept climbing.

What a mess.

I adjusted my mask over my eyes. There was nothing to do but grab on with the others and try to straighten ourselves out as we flew. The helicopter threw up a swirling torrent of water as it roared toward me.

As the rotor wash of the helo approached Hall, I could make out only three bodies clad in black wetsuits hanging on to the same twisted ladder. Hall was swallowed by the rotor wash, and the helo swept toward me. I kept my eyes on the ladder as the whine of the engines grew louder still, and the mechanical storm approached.

I readied myself and . . .

. . . found myself floating in a suddenly calm San Diego Bay.

I thought I'd missed my grab, and I punched the water in anger.

Above me the helicopter climbed to thirty, forty, fifty feet, with two of our men still clinging to the ladder.

One of them—Lucas, a former marine and the only African American in my boat crew—let go. I watched him fall through the air, his arms spinning, until he brought them to his side and crashed into the bay. The other man, who turned out to be Greg Hall, still clung to the ladder.

I later learned that after Hall grabbed on and as the helicopter approached me, one of its engines failed. The helo came a foot or two from crashing into the bay, and the pilots turned to make an emergency run back to Naval Air Station North Island.

The instructors had yelled at Lucas to jump—he was safer in the water than in a disabled helicopter—and so Lucas let go of the ladder and plunged into the bay.

But as Lucas jumped, the twisted ladder righted itself, and hanging on to the bottom was Greg Hall. Now the helo soared to eighty feet, then to one hundred. The instructors yelled to Hall, "Hold! Hold! Hold!"

Later Hall told me that as he watched the world below him whip by at sixty knots from over 150 feet in the air, he looked up at the instructors yelling, "Hold! Hold!" and thought, *Well, no s—t!*

Hall held on to the ladder as the helo flew over the two-hundred-foot-high Coronado Bridge, and I can only imagine what those morning commuters thought when they looked through their windshields, coffee in hand, and saw stuntman Hall flying overhead. Hall had a wild ride, but he and the helo landed safely back at North Island.

Throughout BUD/S, whenever we failed to do something we should have done, we had to do pushups. If you should have sharpened your knife but failed to do so, you did pushups. If you should have inspected your life jacket for saltwater corrosion but hadn't, you did pushups. As Hall walked away from the helo, the instructors yelled, "Hall, drop down!"

Hall dropped into the pushup position.

"Hall, you should have died. Do pushups for being alive."

Greg Hall knocked out twenty happy pushups and yelled, "Hooyah for being alive!"

DROWN-PROOFING

I stood with five other men next to the ledge of the combat training tank as our swim buddies tied our feet together so we could not kick free. We then put our hands behind our backs, and our swim buddies tied our hands together.

"How's that?" my swim buddy asked.

"Feels good."

He tugged at the knot to check it a final time. A knot that came undone meant automatic failure. The five of us on the pool deck exchanged nervous glances, and then, with our feet tied together and our hands tied behind our backs, we jumped into the pool.

It was time for drown-proofing.

The first test was to swim fifty meters. We dolphin-kicked toward the other end of the combat training tank, rolling to our sides every few kicks to catch a breath. After that it was time to "float." Using a small dolphin kick, we floated about a foot below the surface, kicking up to the surface for air every twenty seconds or so.

After five minutes of this, our instructor yelled, "Now bob!"

I blew the air out of my lungs and sank nine feet to the bottom of the pool along with the other men around me. As I felt my feet hit bottom, I crouched into a squat, then pushed off hard. Shooting up through the water, I blew all the remaining air out of my lungs, and as soon as my head broke the surface, I inhaled for an instant and then began to sink again.

I wasn't the strongest swimmer in my class, and I felt a lot more comfortable on land than in water. But I'd learned the importance of staying calm and keeping my mind as focused as possible. If I thought about my bound feet or struggled to free my hands, I'd be in trouble.

Timing was also key. A mistimed breath could mean swallowing water, which could lead to panic, which could lead to forgetting to blow all the air out of my lungs. If that happened, I ran the risk of being stuck too far from the surface of the water to breathe and too far from the bottom of the pool to push myself back up again.

I'd learned from experience that drown-proofing required intense concentration. During training one day before the test, they bound our hands but told us only to press our feet together to simulate them being bound. As we bobbed, my thoughts wandered for a moment. I mistimed a breath, swallowed water, and went sputtering back to the bottom of the pool. I pushed hard for the surface, but I was out of breath. Adrenaline coursed through me, and my mind ran in circles of fear.

I pulled my feet apart and treaded water, gulping air.

"Whatsa matter, Greitens? Oh no, looks like we got another officer panicking on us."

I took a breath to calm myself and let my body sink back down again to the bottom of the pool. I knew that if I focused, I could take charge of my body and mind again.

We all gained confidence with each passing day. Not only were we still alive and still at BUD/S, but we learned we had a team we could count on. We learned that we could do things we might once have thought were impossible.

A REAL FROGMAN

We all came to BUD/S for different reasons. Some sought the respect of parents and friends. Some were inspired by books or movies — even by video games. Some wanted to impress girls. And some just wanted to test themselves. No matter why we joined, we couldn't pass through the tough training without learning more about ourselves than we could have imagined.

Many of the guys grew up in a culture where they'd inherited ideals about manhood from beer commercials and sitcoms. And whether the men they saw on TV were portrayed as overgrown and selfish boys, or as wimps and goofballs, the men who came to BUD/S knew — even if they didn't articulate it — that there had to be more to being a man than that. They wanted to earn something, to pass through a test. They wanted to become strong and worthy.

Every now and then, we ran north of the BUD/S compound and onto the civilian beach in front of the Hotel del Coronado, a popular vacation spot. One day during one of these runs — we still had about sixty men in the class, and we were sick of looking at each other—the bikini-clad women lying out on the beach captured our attention.

Senior Chief Salazar led the run that morning. Senior Chief was a shorter man, powerfully built, who had a long history of honorable operations in the SEAL teams. He was also the epitome of an excellent trainer, unapologetically demanding and relentlessly positive. Every man in our class admired him.

I suspect he knew this, and he used his power to teach important lessons, not just about combat, but also about life.

That day on the beach, he slowed up a little. "You know what, guys?" he said. "I want to tell you something about women. And I want to tell you something about what it means to be a real frogman. You know how a real frogman treats women?"

We listened.

"If you're a real frogman," he said, "then every time a woman leaves your side, she'll feel better about herself."

I thought about that as we continued our run, leaving behind the girls in bikinis and turning our focus back to the training ahead. In a culture where so many had been fed a steady diet of shallow macho posturing that involved degrading women, here was a simple message: "Every time a woman leaves your side, she should feel better about herself." The message felt similar to what Earl had taught: being strong meant being able to do good, to lift up and protect those whose lives you touched.

Many men had come to BUD/S to learn what it meant

to be SEALs. In the process, many of them also learned what it meant to be men. Not every guy embraced Senior Chief Salazar's message, just as not every guy embraced the concepts of teamwork or integrity taught by the SEALs. But every one of us who came to BUD/S was given the opportunity to learn and to take with them a better way to walk in the world.

SUH

I'd been dreading the fifty-meter underwater swim test for months. But I knew waiting wasn't going to make the pool any shorter, so I stood with one of the first groups. Five of us lined up on the pool deck at the deep end of the combat training tank. Five instructors treaded water in front of us. The water was fifteen feet deep, and the pool was twenty-five meters—more than eighty-two feet—across. Our task was straightforward: jump in the pool and execute a front flip, then swim underwater to the other side of the pool and back again, for a total swim of fifty meters underwater.

Standing on the pool deck, my mind started to race: should I jump in as far as possible and save myself an extra foot of swimming, or would that use too much energy and oxygen? Should I do the front flip as soon as I hit the water, or wait until I sank a few feet?

I felt the eyes of the men in my class on my back. They watched me because I was a class leader, and because I was one of the first to swim. They could learn from any mistakes I made.

I grabbed control of my thoughts and tried to concentrate

on only three things: take a deep breath before I jumped, go deep, and stay relaxed while I swam.

I took a very long, very slow, very deep breath, and I jumped. I did the front flip immediately and swam for the other side of the pool at a steep angle, trying to get as deep as I could as quickly as possible. I knew that the deeper you go, the higher the partial pressure of oxygen is in your system. It's actually easier to swim fifty meters at fifteen feet deep than to swim the same distance at five feet deep. So I went deep, and I pulled, kicked, and glided about three inches above the bottom of the pool.

As I came to the turnaround at twenty-five meters, I touched the wall, set my legs, and pushed. The water rushed past me, but the other side of the pool looked very far away, and I was out of air.

Panic threatened to rise, but I told myself, *Thousands of men have done this before you. Thousands more will follow.* As I put my hands out in front to start the next stroke, I thought, *Stay . . .* —and as I pulled my arms back, I completed the mantra—*relaxed.* I repeated this as I swam.

Stay . . . relaxed.

Stay . . . relaxed.

A few more strokes, and I reached the other side of the pool. An instructor launched me onto the pool deck as I touched the finish wall, and I crashed onto the deck between two other students, each of us on our hands and knees, breathing hard.

A corpsman bent down and looked in my eyes. I said, "I'm okay."

"Good job, sir."

That was it? That was the swim I'd worried about for months?

I stood and walked over to my boat crew. "Guys." I took another deep breath. "Just go deep and stay relaxed on the way back. We can all do this."

The guys looked up at me and nodded, but I'm sure it wasn't the most inspiring speech they'd ever heard.

A few minutes later, one of the instructors said, "Oh my, folks, looks like we've got a funky chicken."

When underwater and desperate for oxygen, your body will sometimes start convulsing. It's awkward and painful. Sometimes, the spasming and jerking continues even when you've made it out of the water. One of the men in my group was doing the "funky chicken" on the pool deck.

That morning a very quiet man named James Suh had joined my crew. He looked nervous watching the other man convulse.

I said, "You too, Suh. You got this."

He looked at me. "I got it, Mr. G."

And Suh did get it. He aced the fifty-meter swim that day, and while the class shifted and changed around us for months, Suh remained part of my platoon or boat crew for well over a year. I never once heard him raise his voice. He was utterly dependable, and he was one of the smartest men in our class. He would later help dozens of his fellow classmates with dive physics, and if it hadn't been for Suh's tutoring, many of our men wouldn't have passed the tests that required us to calculate the explosive power of demolitions. Suh was as good on the rifle range and underwater as he was in the air under a parachute. He knew how to fight, and he could fight when he needed to, but he never provoked violence. We went through a lot together, and we became good friends.

Suh would later die as a Navy SEAL in Afghanistan. He was flying on a helo shot down by the Taliban in the middle of a firefight. He was flying in to rescue another man—Matt Axelson, "Axe"—who also sat with us on the pool deck that day.

Sometimes I think about that day, about how he was scared but got the job done anyway.

"I got it, Mr. G," I hear him say.

Yes, Suh. Yes, indeed.

PURE STEEL

Hell Week approached.

Training up to this point had been a challenge, but Hell Week is the hardest week of the hardest military training in the world. We all knew we'd never been tested in the way that Hell Week would test us.

In the classroom, Instructor Harmon said:

"Each one of you is like an earthen vessel—a beautiful piece of pottery—prettied up by your fathers and mothers and teachers with tender loving care. In a few days, Hell Week is going to begin, and we're going to take every one of you out onto the grinder, and we're going to smash you on the ground, break you open, and we're going to see what's inside each one of you. With many of you, we'll find nothing. You are empty men without substance.

"For others, when you break, we're going to have to turn away from the smell, because you live in a weak culture that has allowed you to get by on charm and pretty talk and back-slapping, and you have practiced dishing manure for so long that it almost seeps out of your every pore, and now that's what you are. For others, when we smash you, we'll find inside a sword made of pure Damascus steel. And you are going to become Navy SEALs."

I thought back to my childhood reading, to my first heroes and to the long line of people I'd admired. I imagined each of them forged from Damascus steel, and I hoped that when Hell Week cracked me open, they'd find the same in me.

We arrived at the base early that weekend for a nerve-racking wait. Men brought their favorite movies and music to pass the time. They brought civilian clothes to wear in the event that they quit and were sent home. They carried pillows to sleep on and food to eat. One guy's wife had made oatmeal raisin cookies, and we picked morsels out of the foil. We knew that we'd be burning close to 8,500 calories a day. We also knew that the ocean temperature was in the fifties, and that the body burned calories to produce heat. We ate as much as we could. As night came, we sat up talking.

Men drifted off to sleep, each with his own thoughts. I rehearsed our plan in my mind. As a boat crew leader, my most immediate responsibility was for six other men. I'd instructed our crew to sleep fully dressed, boots on. We knew we'd wake to chaos — instructors firing automatic weapons, artillery simulators exploding, sirens, bullhorns — and our plan was simple: Drop to the ground and crawl out under the east side of the tent. Stay down. I would get a full head count. Hall would grab the back of my collar, the man behind him would grab Hall's collar, and so on, until we were all connected. We couldn't plan to be able to hear each other, and if they threw smoke grenades we might not even be able to see each other. Other men and instructors would be running and crashing around us. Connected, we'd start to move.

I'd briefed my guys. "This week is going to bring a lot of pain we can't avoid. Whatever comes, we'll stay strong and we'll keep smiling. We'll have fun with it, because every moment that passes is a moment that takes us closer to becoming SEALs. We'll work together, and we'll remember we're in this together. But we're also going to be smart, and whenever there's pain we *can* avoid, we're gonna do a little sidestep."

Now I wondered, *Is there anything else I should say? Anything else I should do?*

The cultures I'd read about in school flashed through my mind: the Spartans, the Romans, the Knights of the Round Table. From ancient Jewish tribes to Native American cultures — all of them offered some orderly set of trials that marked a boy's progress into manhood. I thought about Earl Blair in the Durham boxing gym, constructing trials for boys who otherwise might have tested themselves in gangs or on the streets.

We'd all come to BUD/S for many reasons, but I felt we all wanted to be tested. We wanted to prove ourselves worthy. And now here was our chance.

Almost as soon as I fell into sleep, I woke to the sound of a Mark-43 squad automatic weapon. A blank round is not nearly as loud as a live one, but when the gun is rocking just feet away from your ears in an enclosed tent, it still sounds painfully loud.

I rolled to the ground. For a moment — certainly less than a second — I was on my knees and elbows in the sand, about to crawl out of the tent. A huge smile broke across my face. The wait was over. The test had begun.

YOU: SURVIVING HELL

You stand in freezing water up to your chest. Every muscle in your body throbs with pain. You are exhausted beyond anything you could ever imagine, and all around you the night air carries the curses and groans of other men who are gutting it out like you, who are trying to survive the night.

Most won't.

You know the statistics: Maybe one in ten will make it through this week, will survive the hours—days—of punishment required to become a Navy SEAL.

The water is dark around you, but you can make out lights on the beach. You remember your instructors' words as the sun drifted toward the horizon, their voices booming over the bullhorns:

"Say good night to the sun, gentlemen, say good night to the sun."

"Tonight is going to be a very, very long night, gentlemen."

You imagine another hundred hours of this. You see yourself plunging over and over into the icy water, pulling yourself out again. You imagine endless repetitions of sit-ups, flutter kicks, pushups. Surf torture, they call it, when they leave you in freezing water. Not just for a few minutes but for five more days. Five days of struggle and uncertainty. Five days of physical and emotional torment made to separate the iron-willed from the merely strong.

In the distance, a bell sounds three times. And then another three times. As you hear the bell, you know that another student has chosen to quit.

A voice rises and falls, taunting you, inviting you to do the same. "Quit now, and you can avoid the rush later. It just gets colder. It just gets harder."

One by one, sometimes in clusters, other students surrender. All around you, they slog up out of the water, bodies shivering, clothes soaked. They climb up out of the ocean, walk up the sand hill. And they ring the bell.

For them, it is the end.

The others in your crew struggle along with you, and it's their companionship and their strength that buoys you. You are there for each other. You're a team, and you don't want to quit on your team.

But you are bone-tired and shivering. You're afraid you'll never make it through this night, let alone an entire week.

On shore stands a brightly lit tent. Others are gathered inside, their palms cupping mugs of warm coffee. They are wrapped in blankets, eating hamburgers. They are safe.

You could be one of them.

All you have to do is rise out of the icy water and walk toward the tent. It's easy. Students have been doing it all night. Just get up. Get out. Walk toward that bell and quit.

Then you could be warm and dry like the others. Then your stomach could be full, and you could feel your fingers and toes again.

All you have to do is get up, get out. Ring the bell.

What do you do?

PUSHING OUR LUCK

The plan worked perfectly. The seven of us crawled out the side of the tent, avoiding the packs of instructors waiting at the entrance and exit. The night was dark, and in the confusion we felt unseen.

We had a few precious seconds to make sure we were all together. I stood, Hall's hand on my collar, and we ran.

Instructors yelled at us, "Drop!" "Drop!" "Drop down!" but I kept running. Air-raid sirens blared, artillery simulators exploded, guns ripped through endless rounds of ammunition, and I decided to use the chaos of the night to our advantage.

Students were being corralled into the famous concrete compound known as the grinder for a brutal session of physical training under the assault of hoses and prowling instructors. The intention of the instructors was to start Hell Week in chaos. Break the teams apart. Sow confusion. As the seven of us ran for the grinder, I turned left and ducked us behind a Dumpster, where all seven of us crouched to a knee.

The instructors screamed, guns fired, and the other boat crews ran back and forth.

"Mr. G, what are we doing?" We weren't swimming in the river of craziness around us, and it was actually the calm that made some of my guys nervous.

"Be cool," I said. "We're just gonna hang here for a bit."

One of the guys, Raines, said, "My man, this is beautiful." We waited.

"Stay low." I peered around the side of the Dumpster: clear. I stood and we ran back to the beach.

We seven stood on the beach together, catching our breath. No instructors. Then we started to laugh. It was the laugh of the happy nervous. *Was this really happening?*

We listened as sirens blared, whistles shrieked, and smoke grenades spread a menacing pall over the ground. Speakers had been strung up around the grinder, and they amplified the sound of shrieking air-raid sirens. For added confusion, fifty-gallon barrels exploded with artillery simulators and flash-bang grenades.

Raines, who had started with an earlier class and joined ours after recovering from injury, had told me earlier, "A lot of the officers want to be tough. They get all excited. Go charging into the mouth of the cannon. Get soaked. Get beat. Show everybody how tough they are and start the whole week beat and exhausted." I had decided on a different approach.

We stood there, almost giddy with laughter, for a good ten minutes. A few stars shone through the clouds, and waves rolled up the beach. We kept a loose lookout, but no one came. I felt that we'd pushed our luck about as far as it could go. Pretty soon someone would do a head count, and I didn't want to be caught on the beach and have my crew singled out for torture.

I said to my guys, "Gentlemen, let's go join the party. Stay connected. Hold on tight to the man in front of you. We are about to have a great time."

We ran onto the grinder into a whirling mix of soaked, exhausted men; of chaotic pushups and flutter kicks; blaring sirens and bellowing instructors.

Our crew ran through the chaos, and as we ran we tapped our fellow classmates on the head, a tactic we'd discussed on the beach.

The instructors yelled at us, "What the hell are you doing! Drop down!" and I yelled back, "Hooyah, Instructor Jones," but I kept on running, and we kept on with the head tapping.

"Mr. Greitens, what are you doing?"

"Hooyah," I yelled, and we kept on running.

"Mr. Greitens, what the hell are you doing?!"

"We're doing a head count of the class, Instructor Jones."

The instructors had no idea if we'd been ordered to do a head count by another instructor. They assumed we had, and I was willing to let them assume. My crew kept running around the grinder, tapping other guys on the head.

A few guys in the class got what we were doing, and they jumped up to join us, and soon we had a long line of guys running through hoses and smoke and chaos, tapping other guys on the head.

It's unlikely we had really outwitted the instructors; they knew all of the tricks, and they probably turned a blind eye to what we did. SEALs were supposed to take advantage of chaos, and we felt like we had won the first round. We couldn't avoid 99 percent of the pain coming our way, but we'd avoided a little, and we'd given ourselves a sharp psychological edge. It was a beautiful way for us to start the week.

NICE JOB, MR. G

They'd assigned each crew to an IBS, a small inflatable boat that weighed about a hundred pounds and could hold a crew of seven. It stayed with us through every minute of Hell Week. At mealtimes we left a guard on the boat. Instructors who found unguarded boats would steal oars and deflate spray tubes. Unguarded boats led to beatings.

As we sprinted away from the chaos of the grinder, we picked up our boat, and it bounced on our heads as we ran through the soft sand. Around us, I heard the boat crews on either side of us yelling at each other.

"I told you not to—"

"You need to listen!"

"Shut up and run."

The men were soaked and beaten from their time on the grinder, and now they were uncomfortable under their boats and had begun to snipe at each other.

"Let's be cool," I said as we ran. "We're off to a good start, but the whole week's not gonna be like this. Not everything is going to go our way. Listen, though, to the other boat crews right now, tearing each other up. We're gonna stay positive, stay together, and have fun with this. We can all make it through."

I knew that just as it was important to keep our spirits up, it was even more important that we think of ourselves as a team. We'd get through this together, I thought, or not at all.

As we ran on the soft sand in the middle of the night at the start of the hardest week of the hardest military training in the world, Greg Hall said, "Not bad. Not bad at all, Mr. G. We got this."

A few men had already quit. Our crew was solid, and our confidence grew with each step we ran.

I realized that what Warrant Green had said was true, but it wasn't the whole truth. He was right, of course, that officers were watched closely, and he was right that we had to be at the front and set an example. But he was wrong about BUD/S being harder for officers.

It seemed to me that leading could, in fact, be *easier*. For fear to take hold of you, it needed to be given room to run. As a leader, all the space in your mind was taken up by a focus on your men.

I'd gotten to a point where my senses were attuned to every physical, verbal, emotional, even spiritual tremor in the crew. Who looked like he was about to lose his temper? Who was worried about his kid? Who was limping? Who needed to be coached, cheered up, or challenged?

As we ran down the beach, another one of my guys huffed as we ran, "Nice job back there, Mr. G."

I smiled as I ran. Knowing that the men I led had faith in me was the greatest affirmation I could have asked for. Running that night with my men under our boat at the beginning of Hell Week was one of the greatest nights of my life.

SURF TORTURE

That night the instructors started surf torture. We ran into the ocean until we were chest-deep in water, formed a line, and linked arms as the cold waves ran over us. Soon we began to shiver.

"Let's go. Out of the water!"

We ran out through waist-deep water, and as we hit the beach, a whistle blew. One blast of the whistle, and we dropped to the sand. Two blasts and we began to crawl, still shaking from the cold, until our bodies warmed just past the edge of hypothermia.

Then, "Back in the ocean! Hit the surf!"

Some men quit after the opening session on the grinder. Others quit after the run down the beach, and still others quit after they sent us into the water. It struck me that these men had been yelled at before. They'd gotten soaked, done pushups and flutter kicks, had run on the beach. Every man in the class had endured at least this much before, so it wasn't the physical pain that made them quit. No. They lost focus on what they had to do in the moment, and their fear of this monster—Hell Week—overwhelmed them like a giant wave that had crashed and washed away their sense of purpose.

During whistle drills, I crawled with Raines. One of my favorite instructors, Wade, yelled, "Mr. Greitens, you don't want to crawl on your own? You want to wait for Mr. Raines here? Then both of you hit the surf!"

Raines and I took off for the waves, dove into the cold water, ran back onto the beach, and fell again to the sand.

"I guess you two just don't get it," Wade said. "Hell Week is an *individual* evolution. You two keep trying to work together."

But Wade meant the opposite, of course. Hell Week was a team evolution—only teams could survive—and he wasn't yelling at me and Raines so much as pointing out our example to the rest of the class.

Ordered back to the water, we stood at the ocean's edge. The waves crashed and flowed around our soaked boots. We were told to turn toward the beach, our backs to the waves, and, with arms linked, to lie down. Waves crashed over us.

"Kick your boots over your head and into the sand!" the instructors yelled.

With our legs kicked backwards over our heads and our boots dug into the sand, our breathing was constricted; as each wave crashed over us, we held our breath. It felt both ridiculous and ridiculously hard.

Men stood up shaking, their will collapsed, and walked to the instructors to quit.

The instructors asked, "You sure?"

They always were. Once they let quitting become an option—a warm shower, dry clothes, a return to a girlfriend or wife, an easier job—they had no use for a future of cold and wet and pain and misery. We heard the bell ring—*ding, ding, ding*—as they chose another life.

A ROCK AND A HARD PLACE

At some point we traded our boats for 150-pound logs and did "log PT" on the beach. As a team of seven, we ran down the beach with the log bouncing on our shoulders. We struggled to walk over a fifteen-foot-high sand berm with the logs held at our waists. Straight-armed, we held the logs over our heads, then brought them down to our shoulders, then lowered them to the ground, and then we lifted the logs back up to our shoulders and pressed them up over our heads again. We ran with our log into the ocean to "give it a bath," and then we picked up our soaked, slippery log and ran back out of the water and through the soft sand.

I can hardly describe the physical pain of log PT. Nothing I'd ever done prepared me for it. Not marathon running. Not the toughest drills that Earl had put me through at the boxing gym. Nothing I'd undergone in BUD/S came close to the raw agony I felt as we hauled that log in and out of the water, up and down in the sand.

Muscles didn't just burn; they seared. The pain stripped away ego, revealing your core. This was not really physical training at all; it was spiritual training by physical means.

• • •

At one point as we ran, I thought, *If I had to do this alone, I don't know that I could make it.* I had been pushed to the very limits of my physical and emotional endurance. But there was a guy to my left who was counting on me, a guy to my right who was counting on me, and I knew I could stay strong for them.

After log PT, we grabbed our boat again and ran onto the obstacle course, where we were told to haul our boats over the obstacles. All seven of us worked together to drag our bulky rubber craft up the high wooden walls, across the logs, and over the course. Then we ran our boats back to the water again.

We paddled north for one of Hell Week's most dangerous evolutions: rock portage. Coronado Beach has a large outcropping of jagged black rocks. Waves roll in and crash on the rocks. The objective of rock portage was for us to "insert" our team as if on an operation. We had to land our boat on the rocks, jump out amid the crashing waves, and carry the boat over the rocks to dry land.

During practice for rock portage prior to Hell Week, we had learned that it was essential to time the waves. When we got close, our bowman would jump out of the boat and onto the rocks. He held a rope attached to the bow, and he would attempt to anchor himself in the rocks as we continued to paddle. As the waves rolled in, they could crash with tremendous force; a man trapped between the boat and the rocks was in trouble. The first man I'd met at BUD/S broke his leg during rock portage.

As we paddled north before the landing, we all felt exhausted. This was still the first night of what promised to be a very long week. But rowing in the ocean, away from the instructors, the night grew suddenly peaceful. No one yelled, and for a full twenty minutes we did nothing but row.

And worry. We could control a lot of things — how we worked as a team, whether to quit or to endure. But none of us could control a fierce wave, a tossed boat. No one's muscles were harder than rock. No man's hands could hold back a wave.

I didn't fear injury itself. I'd broken bones before. But I was scared of being rolled out of our BUD/S class, having to spend months recovering. I hated the thought of having to start all over again.

The first two boat crews paddled for the rocks. They landed, and I could see their helmet lights bobbing as they carried their boats up and over the rocks. Now it was our turn.

We paddled. As we closed, it looked like the waves were breaking and crashing before reaching the rocks. The tide was out. If we timed it right, we could hit the sand and then carry our boat over the rocks, rather than having to land on the rocks themselves.

Scrambling over the rocks with our boat, we made it to the other side. There, instructors yelled at us to drop down and then punished us with pushups for a dozen small offenses.

But when we picked our boat back up and started running, I said, "Great job."

One of the guys said, "Thank God," and we ran on, the boat bouncing on our heads. Exhausted after hours of punishment, we felt like the luckiest crew in the world.

Eventually the sky started to lighten. We'd made it through the first night.

STEEL PIERS

We were awake and under near-constant assault for the first eighteen hours of Hell Week. We endured long timed runs, marathon swims, more pushups—more everything.

My swim buddy and I knew we were going to freeze all week, so we decided to dive into the waves rather than walk in. They could torture us. But, we thought, we'd show them; we would act like we *enjoyed* it. *You want to freeze us? Ha! We'll freeze ourselves.*

Prior to Hell Week, we'd all dreaded our marathon swims. But now swimming two miles in the ocean was relatively pleasant. Our bodies were warmed by the exercise, and though the instructors patrolled the pack of swimmers in kayaks and yelled at us with bullhorns, they couldn't inflict much pain on us while we swam.

Still, men continued to quit as the day wore on. Two quit after the swim. When they announced that we were going to put on forty-pound rucksacks and march, two more men quit, and then it turned out that we didn't even do the rucksack run. Instead, we were ordered to our boats and then ran to chow.

One of my favorite guys in my crew, Eddie Franklin, would

joke about quitting. "I'm quitting today for sure. Right after the run. Then I'm gonna go up to Pacific Beach and surf and hang out and eat tacos." We'd finish the run, and Eddie would say, "Hey, anybody want to quit with me after breakfast? I gotta eat, but then I'm gonna quit." And he'd go on and on and on like this—sometimes to the annoyance of others who were much closer to actually quitting.

But in Eddie's humor was wisdom. What he reminded you was: I can always quit later if I have to, but right now I can do what I have to do—hold this log over my head, or sit in the freezing surf, or run down the beach with the boat bouncing on my head—for at least ten more seconds. That's really all I have to do: get through the next ten seconds.

After the first night, we got four meals a day: breakfast, lunch, dinner, and midrats—midnight rations—and I set my mind to just surviving from meal to meal. At lunch on Monday, Friday felt years away. But dinner wasn't so far off.

We ran into the chow hall that day already showing signs of wear. Our feet were swollen. Our hands were swollen. They hosed us down before we went inside, but still we had sand in our hair and in our ears and around the collars of our T-shirts.

As we sat down to lunch, we had little energy and less patience. Two guys bumped trays, and glasses of water crashed to the floor. "Watch what you're doing!"

Tempers flared, and we tried to diffuse the tension with humor.

Someone at our table asked, "D'you see Instructor Jones with that bullhorn? He looks like he wants to eat it."

"He loves that thing."

204 — ERIC GREITENS

"Is he single?"

"Yeah."

"No, he's not. He's married to the bullhorn."

"He's probably got a bunch of pet names for it. Oh, bully, oh, bully, oh, bully."

We chuckled and turned back to our food. It didn't matter if what we said was actually funny or mature or even made any sense. It was hilarious to us, and just then being able to laugh reminded us: *We can do this.*

We fought our way through Monday afternoon. We endured the tortures, completed the exercises, ran the races. Usually any moment that passed in Hell Week was a good moment, but we still had Monday night hanging over us. Monday night was infamous. The hardest night of all. Tonight we had the brutal "steel piers."

As the sunlight weakened, the instructors ran us out to the beach. We stood there in a line, and as we watched the sun drift down, they came out on their bullhorns:

"Say good night to the sun, gentlemen, say good night to the sun."

"Tonight is going to be a very, very long night, gentlemen."

They reminded us that tonight was going to be our first full night of Hell Week.

"And you have many, many more nights to go."

We watched the sun slip lower and make contact with the ocean.

Then, when they really wanted to torture us, they said, "Anybody who quits right now gets hot coffee and doughnuts. Come on, who wants a doughnut? Who wants a little coffee?"

As we watched the sun slip away, something broke in our class. Out of the corner of my right eye, I saw men running for the bell. First two men ran, and then two more, and then another. The instructors had carried the bell out with us to the beach. I could hear it ringing:

Ding, ding, ding.

Ding, ding, ding.

Ding, ding, ding.

Over and over, I heard the series of three rings that meant someone had given up. A whole group of guys quit together. We'd begun with 220 students. Only twenty-one originals from Class 237 would ultimately graduate with our class. I believe more men quit at that moment than at any other time in all of our BUD/S training.

Who would have thought that after having to swim fifty meters underwater and endure drown-proofing and surf torture and the obstacle course and four-mile runs in the sand and two-mile swims in the ocean and log PT and countless sit-ups and flutter kicks and pushups and hours in the cold and the sand that the hardest thing to do in all of BUD/S training would be to stand on the beach and watch the sun set?

When I thought about it later, the power of fear hit me full force. As the sun set, men's minds went into overdrive as they anticipated the pain to come. They stood on the beach, perfectly at ease, reasonably warm, but they looked forward, to the tough long night, to the cold and the pain. Their fear built and built and built until they found their release in ringing that bell.

Some handled fear with humor. Some with anger. Others simply didn't give fear a place to roost in their minds. I'd learned to recognize the feelings and think, *Welcome back, fear. Sorry I don't have time to spend with you right now,* and I'd concentrate on helping my teammates.

"How's your foot?"

"Fine."

"Good. Keep an eye on it. Tonight's gonna be a good night for us. Dinner should be pretty soon."

Others just focused on the moment. What a pretty sunset. This is all I have to do to make it through Hell Week right now? Stand on the beach? This is great.

Finally, the bell stopped ringing, and the night was upon us. We formed into boat crews and started running again. The steel piers were located on the San Diego Bay side of the Naval Compound. The water was calm and cold and dark, and we jumped in wearing boots and cammies. We all spread out and began to tread water.

The cold grabbed hold of my bones as the instructors yelled, "Now take off your T-shirts and blouses."

Treading, I yanked off my T-shirt and camouflage top and threw them onto the steel piers.

"Boots!"

My crew and I struggled in the cold water as we untied our boots, teeth chattering and hands shaking. We threw them onto the piers.

"Out of the water!"

We climbed up on the quay wall and stood, feet numb with cold, on the concrete.

"Pushups!"

I felt my blood begin to flow again.

"Get down to the piers!"

I stood on the piers. The instructors were oddly silent, and I could hear the sound of men's teeth chattering all around me.

A voice came over the bullhorn. "Some of you might be here because you thought being a SEAL was cool or glamorous. You thought you could be tough, could be Hollywood. You should know right now that *this* is what being a SEAL is about. A whole lot of misery. You can leave here and go on to serve your country in a lot of other ways. You don't all need to be SEALs."

Men had been doing this for over forty years, I thought. Now it was my turn. This was the culmination of a lot of hard work and of choosing the path I wanted to take. Earl used to say, "Any fool can be violent." Warriors are warriors not because of their strength, but because of their ability to apply strength to good purpose. That's why I was here. This was my test. It was making me stronger, and with this strength I could serve others.

KING OF THE HILL

The night went on.

One evolution, "Lyon's Lope," consisted of a series of cold runs and swims in the bay. Then we ran over to the combat training tank. As we ran, the instructors reminded us that a man had died in the pool just a few classes ago. "Anybody want to quit now?" Of course we all remembered that, and of course it affected us. But we all kept running.

We broke into teams and did caterpillar races across the pool. After the races, the instructors sent a crew out to grab several of the boats. We threw the boats into the pool, and the instructors told us to climb in. As we sat floating in our boats in the pool, an instructor held up a bag of McDonald's hamburgers.

He grinned and said, "King of the Hill. If you get thrown out of your boat, swim to the side of the pool; you're out. Last man standing wins his crew a bag of burgers. Ready. Begin."

Everything started out friendly. We were a class, a team, and while we'd wrestle, we weren't going to hurt or exhaust each other for a burger. But as men were thrown out of the boats, the battle intensified.

The boats could barely bear the weight of all the men fighting. I was wrestling and trying to keep my balance when I heard, "Franklin!" then, "Franklin!" then ten seconds later, "Franklin, help me!"

I looked around and was shocked to see Greg Hall's face underwater, his eyes bulging. Greg was a Division I collegiate football player and one of the strongest men in our class. But in the melee, he had been forced to the bottom of our boat, and now five or six men struggled on top of him, oblivious to his position.

The boat had taken on water, and Greg was pinned to the bottom. As the men fought, the weight in the boat shifted back and forth, which allowed Greg to grab a quick breath and yell before being pushed back under the water. Franklin wrestled beside him, but in the commotion he didn't hear Greg.

I grabbed Greg by the shirt and tried to yank him up, but both his arms were pinned. Two men straddled his chest and another two were fighting on his legs. I couldn't move him.

I erupted. "Get the f—k off! Get the f—k off!"

Wildly, I grabbed a man and shoved him into the water.

I think it's fair to say that I had a reputation for calm. Raines used to say, "Mr. G's cooler than the other side o' the pillow. That man's cooler than a fan." So when the guys saw me explode like that, many of them backed away or dove into the pool—not because they feared me, but because my rage made it obvious that something had gone very wrong.

I pulled Greg Hall up, and he hacked the water out of his lungs. After a moment, I realized we were the last two men in the boat.

Red-faced, one of the instructors hollered, "Mr. Greitens, get over here. Get over here right now!"

I jumped out of the boat and swam to the side of the pool. As I pulled myself out, the instructor grabbed me by my camouflage shirt and threw me against the wall. "What the hell is the matter with you? What are you doing?!"

I started to speak, but the instructor yanked me toward him and then slammed me against the wall again.

From his perspective, it looked like I'd gone crazy for burgers and started attacking my men. I explained that Hall had been trapped at the bottom of the boat. They called Greg over, and he confirmed what had happened.

The instructor shook his head. "All right, you two, go eat a f—kin' hamburger. But just one. You don't get the whole bag."

THE HARDEST MOMENT

Tuesday and Wednesday and Thursday passed in a blur. Days on end. More cold. More running. Endless surf torture.

One night we dug a pit in the sand with our oars, and they let us rest for fifteen minutes at the bottom of the pit. We then built a fire, and in an insane game, the instructors had us run circles around the fire until we were warm, then made us run down to the ocean and jump in, after which we ran back to the sandpit. Imagine a hot tub near the snow. Jumping in the snow is fun once. The hundredth time, not so much.

As our minds grew foggy, the instructors chased us through the night with a bullhorn that played an incessant laugh track. We paddled our boats north, then south. We ran to chow and we ate. Then we hurried through the medical tent for a quick check. And we stayed soaked.

My hardest moment came at what should have been the easiest time. Our crews were gathered at the dip bars (parallel bars where we did exercises to build our triceps). A man from each crew competed, and the winning team was allowed to run to the general-purpose tents on the beach for a rest. It was

Wednesday. We'd been up for three nights straight. We were so tired that men fell asleep standing up. My crew lost.

We ran into the tent last. Sleep—I thought—would be immediate and blissful. I collapsed onto a cot, expecting to pass out instantly, but I found myself wide awake. I shut my eyes and took a long breath through my nose. *That* should put me out.

Nope.

My left foot had been bandaged on my last trip through medical and with each pump of my heart I felt the blood pulse in my foot as if it were wrapped in a tourniquet.

I sat up. Everyone else was asleep. I took off my boot, unwrapped my foot, and threw the bandage to the ground. I put my boot back on and laced it up, knowing that if I slept with my boot off, my foot would swell so badly I'd never get the boot back on.

Frustrated, I lay back on the cot. The sun lanced through an open flap in the ceiling of the tent, and the beam of hot sunlight landed right on my chest and face. After a week of freezing, the tent packed with bodies was now oppressively hot. I sat up again. I tried to move my cot, but I was wedged between two men who were dead asleep. I was stuck.

And pissed. This wasn't fair. The medics had bandaged my foot badly. I had the worst cot. Everyone else was asleep. *What if I can't sleep? Will I make it?* My mind churned out one fearful thought after another. I stood and walked out of the tent.

Two of the guards saw me. "You all right, sir?"

"Yeah, I'm fine."

But I wasn't. The week, though punishing, had been going

well, but I needed this sleep and I couldn't get it. Would they let me sleep later? No. What a stupid question. What was I going to do, ask for a nap? How could I sleep? Should I go somewhere else? No, I had to sleep in the tent. What if I couldn't sleep?

I walked over to a faucet mounted on a wall at about shoulder height. The last thing I wanted was to be wet again, but I twisted the faucet with a sandy, swollen hand. Water poured out and I stuck my head in, letting it wash over my head. It cooled me, and I took a deep, steadying breath.

If I can deal with everything else, I can deal with this. I'm going to be fine.

For a moment, as I walked back to the tent on swollen legs, I had an overwhelming feeling of gratitude. So many men had quit. So many men had been injured. I was over halfway through now, and at this very moment I had been granted an opportunity that almost no one ever received. I had a moment of absolute calm, completely to myself.

"Thank you, God," I said, and I went back into the tent and fell asleep.

When I reflect back on it now, I realize that my hardest moment was also the only time in all of Hell Week when I was alone, focused on my own pain. It was the only moment when I began to think that things were unfair, when I started to feel sorry for myself.

We woke to chaos. They might have been firing blanks again, or it could have just been screaming and bullhorns. We stumbled into the sun, and they made us run for the surf.

Most of the men in the class were still half-asleep and

clumsy and tight and pained. When we were shoulder-deep in water, they told us to run south. We ran an awkward floating race in the ocean, making little progress.

All the warmth in my body fled. I looked back, and the faces of the men in my class wore expressions of pain. I can't remember if I started to sing a song or yell for our class or shout defiance at the instructors, but I remember booming at the top of my lungs, and the class joining me in an outburst of some kind. The attitude of the class turned—as if we all decided to stand up at once after being knocked down—and soon we were shouting with joy.

That was the moment of my greatest personal victory over Hell Week.

HOKEY POKEY

After several days without much sleep and our mental faculties deteriorating rapidly, the instructors began to toy with us. Once, we limp-ran to the beach, and our instructors yelled, "Line up for the Hokey Pokey. Put your left leg in, put your left leg out, put your left leg in, and you shake it all about."

A few guys were less than enthusiastic about this, which gave rise to one of the most ludicrous threats I've ever heard: "You guys better shape the hell up and get serious about this Hokey Pokey!"

In my delirium, I couldn't control myself, and I started laughing—hard. I crossed my left arm over my face to muffle the laughter.

"You think this is funny, Mr. Greitens?"

I tried to steady myself, but when I took my arm from my face, I couldn't control myself. "Yes, Instructor."

I thought he'd send me into the surf, and for a moment I worried that he'd make the whole class pay for my laughter, but instead he said, "Well, if you think this is so damn funny, why don't you get up here?!"

I ran to the front of the class.

"Now, Mr. Greitens. You went to Oxford right, and you were a Rhodes Scholar?"

"Hooyah."

"Then you should be pretty damn smart, right?"

I felt like I was being set up, but I didn't know what to do. "Hooyah?"

"Well, then, I want to see the best damn Hokey Pokey I've ever seen, you got it?"

"Hooyah!" I faced the others. "Okay, guys! You put your left elbow in, you put your left elbow out, you put your left elbow in, and you shake it all about. You do the Hokey Pokey, and you turn yourself around . . ." And then—overcome with the joyful absurdity of the moment—I yelled, "AND THAT'S WHAT IT'S ALL ABOUT!" I felt lighter and more relaxed than I had in a week.

I led the class through right elbow in, right elbow out, left foot in, left foot out, and we all began to shout at the end of each turn, "AND THAT'S WHAT IT'S ALL ABOUT!"

When I'd finished, the instructor turned to me. "Mr. Greitens, that was the best damn Hell Week Hokey Pokey I've ever seen. You guys all get five minutes rest."

We sat down next to our boats. We were too tired to joke now, almost too tired to breathe deeply, but as the guys in my crew leaned against the side of our boat and fell immediately asleep, I sat in the sand, very proud of myself. I was not the fastest runner, not the fastest swimmer, not the fastest man on the obstacle course, but at least for the moment, I was the world's greatest living Hokey Pokey Warrior.

MIND GAMES

We learned we could hallucinate and still function. We learned we could take turns passing out and still function. And we learned we could fight off mind games.

The instructors called over one person from each boat crew and gathered them around a wooden board covered with a cloth. They pulled the cloth back to reveal seven objects: a toothbrush, CO_2 tube, penny, safety pin, piece of gum, watch, and 550 cord (a type of string). They gave us thirty seconds to observe and then covered the board and sent us back to our crews to write down what we had seen.

Most of the trainees' memories were impaired: "Penny, and a piece of gum, and . . . and . . . and maybe a watch?"

But other guys would come back and rattle off, "Penny, safety pin, watch, CO_2 tube, toothbrush, did I say watch? Oh, a piece of gum . . ." They were incredibly sharp after five days without sleep.

On Thursday night we ran to our boats, rowed out past the surf zone, and began the around-the-world paddle. Coronado is a peninsula, connected to Imperial Beach by a thin sliver of land. In the around-the-world paddle, we rowed all the way around Coronado. The beginning of our paddle was glorious. We stroked with a fresh shot of adrenaline because we knew this was the last night of Hell Week.

My crew and I paddled hard, but our boat was leaking air. The extra drag through the water slowed us, and we fell to the back of the line of boats.

An instructor yelled at us, "Okay, you guys don't want to put out? Go ahead and chilly dip." We had to jump out of the boat and into the cold bay.

As the boat crew leader, my job was to steer. I used my oar as a rudder, and at one point my guys turned back to me—"Mr. G!"—and woke me up because I'd fallen asleep and turned us off course.

The lights of San Diego swirled as I fought to stay awake. The crew kept at it. None of us could have made it around the island alone, but working together through bouts of consciousness and sleep, we managed to keep moving forward as a team.

As we paddled, some of the chatter had become nonsensical.

"Mr. G, did you see? Did you call those guys?"

"What?"

"The lights of the green and the red sabers, see how they're attacking and bumping each other?"

"What?"

"Oh my God, it's like a squirrel there, and he had the water in him!"

"Martin, wake up!"

We finished the paddle that night. I walked out of chow on Friday morning and thought, *Last day. We made it.*

The instructors played with us: "Prepare to up boat. Up boat. Okay, let's begin walking, gentlemen. Tomorrow'll be your last day of Hell Week, just one more night to go."

Struggling under the boat, one of my guys asked, "Mr. G, it's Friday, right? It's the last day, right?"

"Yeah, yeah, it's Friday, I'm sure." It was, wasn't it? I yelled over to my friend and fellow officer Mike Fitzhugh. "Mike, it is Friday, right?"

"Yeah, I think so."

WHO MAKES IT

The area known as the demo pits is really just one huge hole in the ground surrounded by a fence. During Hell Week, they pumped the hole full of seawater, creating a revolting slurry of muddy salt water, sweat, and greasy bubbles that popped with orange residue.

As we ran into the demo pits, a whistle blew, and we dropped to the ground. Smoke grenades exploded, and artillery simulators boomed. Two whistles blew, and we started to crawl.

The stench of sulfur assaulted me. I blew my nose and caught a wad of purple snot on my sleeve. *Purple snot. Excellent.* We crawled into the pit, immersed up to our armpits in sludge. Two ropes were stretched across the pit, one of them strung about a foot over the scum; the other was five feet higher than that. Our job: to climb onto the ropes and then—with our feet on the bottom rope and our hands on the top rope—inch across the scum pond while the Brown Shirts shook the ropes.

I knew from Hell Week lore that this was the last evolution of the week. As my fellow students climbed across the ropes, I sat in the disgusting muddy water, the sun beaming, and I was very, very happy. Hell Week was about to end. I'd made it. We'd made it.

A whistle blew. Then two whistles.

The instructors called, "Get back to your boats. Get back to your boats. Paddle down to the compound."

I crawled out of the pit, my mind reeling. Were they serious? Weren't we finished? Anger lashed through my haze of exhaustion. *These instructors screwed up! We were supposed to finish back there; they don't know that we're supposed to be done!*

We ran to our boats, paddled out through the waves, then rowed north back to the compound. My crew was running on frayed nerves. "What the f—k is this! What the f—k!"

I didn't know. I couldn't believe it.

When we had rowed to the compound, the instructors started to beat us again. "Hit the surf, go get wet and sandy."

We could no longer dive into the ocean. We simply fell over in the water, got soaked, and then fought our way back to our knees and limped back onto the beach. We held on to each other to keep standing.

"Drop down! Face the ocean!" They made us do pushups, and then the instructor yelled, "Recover."

When we stood and turned around, every instructor and all of the SEAL staff of the Naval Special Warfare Compound stood in a line atop the sand berm.

The commanding officer called down to us. "BUD/S Class 237, you are secured from Hell Week!"

Really?

We looked down at our boots, up at the instructors. Was this a trick? Then Franklin leaned back, open-chested, and let out a roar, and we all started to shout.

We turned and hugged each other. We'd made it.

We shook the hands of every one of the instructors, and then we staggered over the sand berm to medical. After a final check, we walked out into the sun and found, laid out for us, two large pizzas and a bottle of sports drink for every man.

I sat on the concrete next to my guys. We were too tired to talk. Too tired to shout. But definitely not too tired to eat. It was the most delicious pizza I've ever had in my life.

People always ask me, "What kind of people make it through Hell Week?" I don't really have an answer to that. I do know—generally—who *won't* make it through Hell Week. The weightlifting meatheads who think the size of their biceps indicates their strength: they usually fail. The kids covered in tattoos announcing to the world how tough they are: they usually fail. The preening leaders who don't want to be dirty: they usually fail. The "me first, look at me, I'm the best" former athletes who've always been told they're stars: they usually fail. The blowhards who have a thousand stories about what they're going to do but a thin record of what they've actually done: they usually fail. The whiners, the "this is not fair" guys: they usually fail.

The vicious beauty of BUD/S is that there are no excuses, no explanations. You do or do not.

It seemed clear to me that the week revealed character, but

didn't transform it. I thought of the stories that people in Bosnia and Rwanda had told me about their neighbors. They'd told me stories about people who took extraordinary risks to save the lives of others; and they'd spoken of those they'd known all their lives who — when tested — abandoned their friends and neighbors. Who could have known?

BUD/S was the same way: who knew until the test came?

After the final medical check, we returned to our barracks. I went to my room and dragged myself to my bed. I sat down on it. I had half a pizza left, and I set the box on the ground. *That'll taste good in the morning, or whenever I wake up. Will I sleep until Saturday?*

I set a pillow at the foot of my bed and kicked my feet up on the pillow. I wanted to keep my feet raised to reduce swelling. I set another pillow behind my head.

I smiled. Hell Week was over. It was the best time I never want to have again.

EVERYTHING CHANGES

After a long, *long* sleep, I rose from my bed. My body felt heavy and numb, but when I held up my hands I saw that the Hell Week swelling had gone down a little. I joined the others, and we shuffled like zombies to medical. There they checked us again for cellulitis (flesh-eating bacteria), pneumonia, and broken bones.

With our medical check passed, we drove to a local restaurant and tore through a breakfast of stacked pancakes, sausages, crispy hash browns, cheesy eggs, sparkling fresh fruit, and biscuits covered in gravy. If last night's pizza had been the best meal of my life, this breakfast came in a close second.

I was still swollen — head, hands, feet — and when I pulled up to my house and stepped out of the car, I moved slowly. My neighbor's sprinkler was on, and just a few drops landed on the sidewalk, but I walked wide around it. I wanted, for a day, to be nothing but warm and dry.

After a blissful weekend off, we jumped right back into training. We did physical drills on the grinder and runs on the beach, and we continued our weekly two-mile ocean swims.

One early Tuesday morning, my swim buddy and I came

out of the ocean, and as we ran up the beach, a man shouted something to us as he passed.

"What did he say?" I asked.

"I don't know. Something about a plane crash in New York."

As the rest of the team finished the swim, we stripped off our wetsuits and donned boots and camouflage uniforms as word passed among us: a plane had crashed into the Twin Towers of the World Trade Center. No, it was two planes. One of the buildings collapsed. Both buildings collapsed. Thousands of people died.

At the chow hall, the TV was on, and we hustled through the line and gathered at the tables near the corner of the hall so that we could watch the news. I could hardly take in what was happening. None of it seemed real. Thousands of people had died? Usually, we bantered while we ate, but that morning we wolfed down our food in silence, except for occasional words of profanity and prayer.

We had sat down for our meal thinking we were members of a peacetime military. When we stood, we knew our class was going to war.

"Mr. G," someone later asked, "you think that they'll speed up our training and send us to Afghanistan?"

In his question, I heard reflected my own desire—to *do* something, to be there for the country's critical hour. Each member of the class in his own way said, "I wish I'd been on one of those planes." It wasn't bravado, and it wasn't just talk. We had signed on to fight for our country, and now the fight was on.

SEALs fight from the sea, from the air, and from the land. We serve as the nation's elite commando force, and suddenly it looked like our country had an immediate need for us. We trained hard, and over the next several months, we were shaped into warriors.

In dive phase, we learned to be combat swimmers. Up to that point, I had never taken a single breath underwater. In this phase of our training, while swimming underwater with scuba gear, we were repeatedly attacked. Instructors jerked our mouthpieces from our mouths, tore off our facemasks, ripped off our fins, flipped us in circles, turned off our air, tied our hoses in knots, and then swam away.

Starving for oxygen underwater, we had to wrestle our twisted tanks and hoses in front of us, turn on our air, untie our hoses, and try to reestablish a line to life-giving oxygen. As soon as we caught a breath of oxygen and straightened our tanks, they hit us again.

Later we swam to the bottom of the combat training tank with a swim buddy, just one scuba tank and one mouthpiece between us and our facemasks completely covered in tape. Both blind underwater, we shared oxygen back and forth as we transferred all of our dive gear from one man to the other. Later they had us tread water for five minutes with our hands in the air while wearing sixty pounds of gear. Anyone whose hands touched the water failed. Dozens of men failed different tests, and our training moved forward without them.

Nine weeks after I first entered dive phase, my swim buddy and I descended into the water at night wearing a Dräger combat diving system that emitted no bubbles. We kicked underwater for several hours, adjusting our course several times according to the dive plan we had built by studying the chart, tides, and currents. Using a series of hand gestures, we communicated underwater and executed our plan until we reached our target, placed our simulated mine, and swam away.

We then moved to land warfare and weapons training. At Camp Pendleton, we fired thousands of rounds from a Sig Sauer 9mm pistol and thousands more from our rifles. Before the military, I'd shot a gun once before. Now I became comfortable using a weapon that was designed to take a life. Eventually, my team and I would run and shoot, shouting and firing hundreds of bullets together, often just feet from each other, trusting the men around us with our lives.

I learned how to shoot a submachine gun, a shotgun, and an AK-47. I fired light anti-armor rockets and anti-tank weapons, and I planted claymore mines. We lined up on the range at night and learned to fire our rifles using night-vision goggles and lasers. We learned how to clear jammed weapons, how to rappel, how to gunfight as a team. We learned how to patrol quietly and how to black out every bit of metal and every piece of gear that might reflect light.

We learned how to navigate over mountains and how to use radios. We spent weeks in the woods, learning the basics of reconnaissance. As a class, they tear-gassed us to teach us that — even in pain and coughing, shrouded by a cloud of gas — we could still fight.

Toward the end of BUD/S, we went to San Clemente Island — "Where no one can hear you scream" — to do a night ocean swim.

The instructors stepped onto safety boats with loaded shot-guns.

"Just thought you should know," said one. "San Clemente is home to one of the largest breeding grounds for great white sharks in the world."

We looked at one another and then at the water. I tried not to imagine the ocean frothing with blood.

"Now get in the water and swim."

I got in. And I swam. Very, very fast.

A LESS-THAN-PERFECT LANDING

Next up: Fort Benning, Georgia, for Army Airborne School, where we'd learn how to jump out of planes. The concept seemed simple to me, but it took three weeks to learn open door, green light, go!

It turns out that parachutes are deceiving. You don't float to the ground, as I'd imagined, but crash, like a human lawn dart.

Every now and then, people ask me if I was afraid during training. I tell them: yes, I was afraid. I was afraid of getting into helicopters and of jumping *out* of helicopters. I was afraid of swimming with the sharks in the ocean at night, afraid I'd fall fifty feet on the obstacle course, afraid during log PT that the log would come down wrong and fracture my neck, afraid during rock portage that I'd mess up and break my ankle.

The truth is that all of us who undergo this training are human; we feel fear — plenty of it. But we also train our bodies and our minds to ignore that fear, to run or swim or jump with it. It's not always easy, but it's necessary. And it's possible.

It was the same on the first day I had to jump out of a plane: sharp, visceral fear.

I'd never really thought about how awkward and constricting it is to have a parachute on your back and a reserve in front. I was strapped in everywhere—over my shoulders, across my back and stomach, between my legs. I wore fatigues, a heavy helmet, and goggles. All I could do was waddle onto the plane with everyone else, sit down, and wait.

As we soared, I drilled myself on the emergency procedures we'd learned. *What if the parachute opens halfway? What if it doesn't happen at all?* I ran through percentages in my head. Not many people had died in the last hundred classes, so the odds were with me. Weren't they? Or did it mean it was time for another disaster?

Our plane rumbled through the air. It was a bright, sunny day for a jump.

Then it was time.

I stood up, hooked a cord from my pack to a steel line in the plane, and shuffled toward the door. When I jumped, the line would pull taut and yank out my chute. "Go!" cried one of the instructors, and I jumped.

The wind rushed around me, and for a frozen second, I could feel it whipping against my camouflage trousers. I heard the whistling *zzzzzzzz* of the static line being pulled taut.

I'd been taught to hold a stable body position and then look up to check that all my lines were straight and that I saw a fully opened canopy above me.

I counted.

I looked up.

And above me my lines were twisted, my parachute not completely open.

Not good. I must have jumped poorly. The wind had turned my body in the air, and the parachute had twisted as it opened.

I reached up, grabbed my risers, cycled my legs in the air, and I pulled the cords apart as I had been trained. The parachute popped fully open.

Catastrophe averted, I had a moment of peace and an extraordinary view. *Wow, this is great,* I thought. And then I remembered I still had to worry about landing.

They'd taught us the specifics of the maneuver called the "parachute landing fall," which was supposed to ensure a smooth landing. You hit the ground with the balls of your feet, then roll to your calves, keep rolling to your hamstrings, then onto your rear end and back. When executed properly, it lessened the impact of crashing into the earth.

The ground rushed up at me, and I tried to execute the move to the best of my ability but felt like I'd just slammed into the ground. I got to my knees in a daze and started to collect my parachute, now depleted on the ground.

One of my guys yelled, "Mr. G, nice parachute landing fall. You crashed feet, ass, head!" Clearly, I still had a lot to learn.

THE TRIDENT

We stood in a nondescript concrete bay known as the boat barn, a single American flag its only adornment. No band, no streamers. We were not in dress uniforms but in starched fatigues. I listened to the words spoken as a golden Trident was pinned over my heart.

"The Trident has been the badge of the Navy SEALs since 1970. It is the only warfare specialty pin that is the same for officers and enlisted. It symbolizes that we are brothers in arms. We train together, and we fight together.

"There are four parts to the Trident. Each one symbolizes an important facet of our warfare community.

"The anchor symbolizes the Navy, the premier force for power projection on the face of the planet and the guarantor of world peace. It is an old anchor, which reminds us that our roots lie in the valiant accomplishments of the Naval Combat Demolition Units and Underwater Demolition Teams.

"The trident, the scepter of Neptune, or Poseidon, king of the oceans, symbolizes a SEAL's connection to the sea. The ocean is the hardest element for any warrior to fight in, but we must be masters of the sea.

"The pistol represents the SEAL's capabilities on land—whether direct action or special reconnaissance. If you look closely, it is cocked and ready to fire and should serve as a constant reminder that you, too, must be ready at all times.

"The eagle, our nation's emblem of freedom, symbolizes the SEAL's ability to swiftly insert from the air. It reminds us that we fly higher in standards than any other force. Normally, the eagle is placed on military decorations with its head held high. On our insignia, the eagle's head is lowered to remind each of us that humility is the true measure of a warrior's strength."[9]

After they pinned a Trident on each of us, we turned as a class, ran down the pier, and jumped into the bay. As a trainee, I had jumped into the water a thousand times. This was the first time I hit the ocean as a Navy SEAL.

We swam across the bay and then ran a six-mile course across the island of Coronado. We finished our run at a beach, where we grilled steaks, told stories, and wished each other well.

Like every great rite of passage, the celebration was also colored by some sadness. I was leaving men who had become brothers. We'd laughed a thousand crazy laughs motoring on the ocean, climbing in the mountains, and before jumping from planes. Standing on the beach, this was our last moment as a class together. I knew that all of us would be deployed, and that some of us might not return.

I'd come to the end of one leg of my journey. I had traveled a tough road with some of the finest men our country, men I knew would remain friends for the rest of my life. Now it was time for a new mission.

IRAQ

I have no memory of when the suicide truck bomb detonated. Lights went out in the barracks. Dust and smoke filled the air. I found myself lying belly down, legs crossed. Men were gasping and coughing around me.

Then the burning started.

The insurgents had packed chlorine into the truck bomb: it was a chemical attack. It felt as if someone had shoved an open-flame lighter inside my mouth, the flames scorching my throat, my lungs. My eyes burned, and I fought to keep them open.

From nearby, Staff Sergeant "Big Sexy" Francis called, "You all right?"

"Yeah, I'm good!" Mike Marise answered. Mike had been an F-18 fighter pilot in the U.S. Marine Corps who walked away from a comfortable cockpit to fight on the ground in Fallujah.

"Joel, you there?" I shouted to my buddy. My throat was on fire, and though I knew that his bunk was only two feet away, my burning eyes and blurred vision made it impossible to see him in the dust-filled room.

He coughed. "Yeah, I'm fine," he said.

Lieutenant Colonel Fisher shouted from the hallway. "You can make it out this way! Out this way!"

We stumbled over gear and debris as shots pierced the morning. My body low, my eyes burning, I felt my way over a fallen locker as we all tried to step toward safety. As gunfire ripped through the air, I stepped out of the east side of the building and fell behind an earthen barrier, Lieutenant Colonel Fisher beside me.

On my hands and knees, I began hacking up chlorine gas and spraying spittle. My stomach spasmed in an effort to vomit, but nothing came. Fisher later said he saw puffs of smoke coming from my mouth and nostrils.

I looked down and saw a dark red stain across my shirt and more blood on my pants. *I'm injured.* I shoved my right hand down my shirt and pressed at my chest, my stomach. I felt no pain, but I knew a surge of adrenaline could mask the pain of an injury.

I patted myself again: chest, armpits, crotch, thighs. No injuries. I pressed my hand to the back of my neck, and when I pulled them away they were sticky with sweat and blood. I still couldn't find an injury.

Finally, I realized, *It's not my blood.*

I couldn't take a full breath; every time I tried to inhale, my throat gagged and my lungs burned. But we had to join the fight. Mike Marise and I ran back into the building. One of our Iraqi comrades stood in the bombed-out stairwell, firing his AK-47 as the sound of bullets ricocheted around the building.

Fisher and another Marine found Joel sitting on the floor in the chlorine cloud, trying to get his boots on. Shrapnel from the truck bomb had hit Joel in the head.

When he'd said, "I'm fine," we'd expected him to follow us out of the building. But instead of standing up and moving, his brain had told him *boots . . . boots . . . boots* as he bled out the back of his head. They pulled Joel out of the building and a medic came to treat him.

Fisher, Francis, and I charged up the twisted bombed-out staircase to higher ground. The truck bomb had blown off the entire western wall of the barracks, and as we raced up the staircase over massive chunks of concrete and debris, we were exposed to gunfire from the west.

Iraqi soldiers from the barracks—our allies—fired away, but I couldn't see any targets. At the top of the stairs, I paused for a break in the gunfire, sucked in a pained, shallow breath, and then ran onto the rooftop.

A lone Iraqi guard stood there, armed with an M60 and ripping bullets to the west. I ran to cover the northwest, and Francis followed to cover the southwest. A burst of gunfire rang out, and I dove onto the rough brown concrete and crawled through a mess of empty plastic drink bottles, cigarette butts, and dip cans—trash left behind by Iraqi soldiers who'd been on guard duty.

I peered over the edge of the roof to check for targets and caught sight of a tall minaret on a mosque to the northeast. It was not uncommon for snipers to take positions inside minarets and shoot at Americans. It would have been a long shot for even the best sniper, but as I scanned the streets, I kept my head moving, just in case.

Below me, women and children scattered in all directions. Far off to the north, I saw armed men running toward the building. I steadied my rifle and aimed. I took a slow breath, focused my sights, laid the pad of my finger on the trigger . . .

No. Those were Iraqi police from our base.

I called to Francis, "You see anything? You have any targets?"

"Nothing."

The sun rose. I felt the heat of the day begin to sink into the roof. I waited. I watched. My breathing was still shallow, and I felt as if someone had tightened a belt around my lungs and was pulling hard, squeezing the air from me. I glanced over the ledge of the roof again.

Nothing.

I considered our situation: We had plenty of bullets, and my med kit was intact. We had the high ground, good cover, and a clear view of every avenue of approach. We'd need some water eventually, but we could stay here for hours if necessary. Sitting there in a nasty pile of trash on the rooftop of a bombed-out Iraqi building in Fallujah, I thought: *Man, I'm lucky.*

A moment later, Travis Manion and two other Marines ran onto the roof. Travis was a recent graduate of the United States Naval Academy, where he'd been an outstanding wrestler. I came to know him while we patrolled the streets of Fallujah together. Travis was tough, yet he walked with a smile on his face.

I glanced at the minaret again. The sky was blue and clear — a beautiful day. The radio crackled with traffic informing us that a Quick Reaction Force of tanks was on its way. After the explosion and the gunfire and the rush of adrenaline, the day grew quiet and hot. Tanks arrived, and a few Humvees rolled in for an evacuation of the injured. Because we'd been in the blast, Francis and I were ordered to leave with the casevac for the hospital.

I called over to Travis: "You got it?"

"Yeah, I got your back, sir."

Later it would strike me how matter-of-fact that had become — one man taking responsibility for another man's life, if only for a moment.

All the armored vehicles were full, so a young Marine and I climbed into the open bed of a Humvee made for moving gear. For armor, two big green steel plates had been welded to its sides. Lying flat, we had about as much cover as two kids in the back of a pickup truck during a water-gun fight. As we drove for the base, we'd be exposed to fire from windows and rooftops. I readied my rifle, prepared to shoot from my back as the Humvee raced through Fallujah, bumping and bouncing over the uneven dirt roads.

When we'd made it out of the city, I turned to the young Marine beside me.

"You okay?" I asked.

He gave me a smirk. "You know what, sir?" he said. "I think I'm ready to head home after this one." Somehow that seemed hilarious to us, and we both laughed our heads off, exhausted, relieved.

At Fallujah Surgical, I was treated among a motley crew of

Americans and Iraqis, many half-dressed, bedraggled, bloody. I asked about Joel, and they told me his head injury had been severe enough that they'd flown him straight to Baghdad.

When I got back to the barracks, I pulled off my boots, peeled off my clothes, and threw my armor in a corner. Everything reeked of chlorine. I stepped into a shower. As the water ran over me, I rubbed my scalp. Down fell tiny bits of concrete from the explosion. I watched as the pieces fell to the shower floor and washed down the drain. *That was close.*

For the next few weeks, I spent every night hacking and coughing in bed. When I woke in the morning and tried to run, my lungs hurt. I felt like they had been zipped half-shut. Still, I ran every day, and eventually I could take a deep, full breath. I lost a bit of my hearing for a few weeks, but it could have been far worse.

Not everyone I served with that day would be so lucky.

GOING HOME

I could hear the *whomp* of the Chinook helicopter's blades before I saw its gray outline appear against the black sky. I stood thirty yards from the airstrip with my bags at my feet. Despite the plugs in my ears, the high-pitched whine of the twin engines was deafening as the helo set down and kicked up a swirling storm of dust. I shook my buddy's hand, picked up my two stuffed duffel bags, and jogged toward the bird.

I felt a familiar buzz of adrenaline as I trotted up the ramp and into the helo. Usually, boarding a helicopter meant moving on to another location, another mission. But this time, it meant I was heading home.

I clipped my bags to the deck of the aircraft and stepped past Iraqi prisoners sitting blindfolded, their hands zip-tied behind their backs. I wondered what was going through their minds. They had been captured, yanked from their homes, and were now on a helicopter for the first time in their lives surrounded by unfamiliar smells and sounds, with no idea where they were headed.

As we flew for Balad, I thought, *This is the last leg of my last trip of my last day in Iraq*. I sat on the port side of the helo, and as we flew, I looked past the gunner out the window onto a black night.

I let my mind drift. I was going to be met in Virginia by a beautiful girl, devilishly smart, warm, with an eyes-over-the-shoulder smile that always made my world brighter. I thought about walking with her down the beach.

Bright red tracer bullets flew past us into the sky. I tensed, expecting some reaction from the crew—a hard banking maneuver, some return fire from the door gunner, but we flew straight ahead, tracers still ripping past us.

Over the past few months, six helicopters had been shot down over Iraq. *Why aren't we evading?* My mind worked to come up with some explanation. *Maybe those are our tracers? But they're too close.* The tracers kept whizzing by, our pilot maintaining his course.

I gritted my teeth. *Not now, on the last leg of my last ride on my last day of this deployment.*

The helicopter banked hard to port. A few more tracers flew past, and the door gunner racked his weapon and pulled the trigger, and bullets barked out at the ground below. *Finally!*

When we landed safely in Balad, I knew that, barring anything bizarre—being hit by a wild mortar round, choking to death on a turkey leg in the chow hall—I'd get home safely.

When I made it to my rack on base, I dropped my duffel bags and took off my body armor. I unbuttoned the left chest pocket of my desert camouflage top and took out a St. Christopher medal given to me by a Catholic friend, a Buddhist prayer scroll from a Buddhist friend, an angel coin from a Protestant friend, a hamsa from a Jewish friend, and a coin imprinted with a Hindu deity from a Hindu friend.

Before the deployment, I'd figured it would be a bad move to turn down any prayers that were offered. I'm not sure which one did the trick, so I said simply, "Thank you, God," as I stepped out of my uniform.

TRAVIS

Once back home in Washington, D.C., I called Joel Poudrier, whose head injury in Fallujah had led to his evacuation all the way to Virginia. I hadn't seen him since the morning of the truck bomb.

When I got him on the phone, Joel said, "They put a ridiculous number of staples in my head, and the Marines are making me go to a psychologist to see if I'm crazy. Problem is, I was nuts before the explosion, so he's got no way to tell if I've changed." We made a plan to get together.

Three weeks later, still trying to find my rhythm at home, I was stepping out of my truck when my cell phone rang.

"Hey, Eric, it's Joel."

Something in his voice sent a shot of dread through me.

"Hey, man, how's it going?"

"I got some bad news."

"Yeah?"

"Travis Manion was killed yesterday in Fallujah."

I stood on the street. A red and white taxi slowed at a stop sign and then accelerated away. The day seemed too normal, too cheerful even, to contain this kind of news.

In my mind, I saw Travis on the day of the suicide truck bomb, pictured him running straight across the compound—rifle in hand and Marines behind him—to aid us. He'd been the first man to join me on the roof.

I remembered getting ready to leave the roof and asking Travis, "You got it?"

"Yeah, I got your back, sir."

"Take care of your people" is one of the principal lessons of military leadership, and my people were not just SEALs or the men in my targeting cell. Serving overseas, everyone in uniform is part of the same team. Everyone is away from his or her family. Everyone is exposed to danger. Everyone endures the same long, hot days, hears the same bad jokes, reads the same old magazines. Everyone loses friends. Everyone misses home.

If we take care of our people on deployment, I thought, *why should that change when we come home?* I didn't know yet what I could do, but the answer would soon reveal itself.

When Joel Poudrier arrived at my apartment, I remembered the last time I'd seen him. That day he'd been kneeling on one knee outside the barracks as a corpsman tended to his bleeding head wound.

We talked about his son's baseball team, his golf game. He was recovering well, and he told me that he wanted to go back to Iraq to rejoin his unit. He bent his neck and showed me the scar where they'd stapled his head back together. I dug my body armor out of a black duffel bag and showed him where the blood—his blood—still stained my armor.

"Can I have that back?"

"You should have ducked," I said. "Do the Manions know we're on our way?"

"Yeah, I called 'em just as I was pulling up here."

Our visit with the Manions was sad but inspiring at the same time. For all their suffering, Travis's family was not consumed by bitterness, rage, or despair. The Manions had lost their only son, yet they impressed me with their desire to honor Travis's life.

On the drive home, Joel and I decided that we'd do something for the Manion family. We would find a way to ensure that Travis's legacy—and the legacy of all those who served and sacrificed—would live on.

Joel pulled his car up to the curb in front of my building. We both stepped out, and I shook his hand and pulled him into a hug.

"Thanks, brother."

As I watched his taillights recede, I thought about the connection between hot, brutal warfare in distant lands and the kind of community spirit we had seen at the Manions' home. I had seen it before in Bosnia, Rwanda, Bolivia, and other places where courageous people found ways to live with compassion in the midst of tremendous hardship. Across the globe, even in the world's "worst places," people found ways to turn pain into wisdom and suffering into strength. They made their own actions, their very lives, into a memorial that honored the people they had lost.

On the frontlines—in humanitarian crises, in wars overseas, and around some kitchen tables here at home—I'd seen that peace is more than the absence of war, and that a good life entails more than the absence of suffering. A good peace, a solid peace, a peace in which communities can flourish, can only be built when we ask ourselves and each other to be more than just good, and better than just strong. And a good life, a meaningful life, a life in which we can enjoy the world and live with purpose, can only be built if we do more than live for ourselves.

THE MISSION CONTINUES

After Joel and I met with the Manion family, I arranged to visit with the wounded at Bethesda Naval Hospital. As I pulled into the hospital parking lot, I thought, *There's only one reason I'm not a patient here: luck*. If the suicide truck bomb had detonated two feet closer, if the shots at the helo had hit their mark, I could have been lying in one of those beds. Or in a coffin.

As I pushed open the heavy brown door to one of the hospital rooms, a young soldier lying in bed caught me and followed me with his eyes as I walked into the room. Gauze bandages were wrapped around his neck. He'd taken a bullet through the throat.

"How you doin'?" I asked.

On a yellow legal pad, he wrote, "Fine, was actually having fun over there before this."

His young wife sat next to him with red-rimmed eyes, her hand on his shoulder. They treated most of the Army's wounded at Walter Reed, but for reasons having to do with his care, they'd brought this soldier to Bethesda.

"You know you're in enemy territory here," I joked.

He smiled and wrote in reply, "Navy actually okay. Some of them."

We communicated a bit more, and as I walked out of his room, I thought, *What's this guy going to do next?*

I walked into another room where a Marine had lost part of his right lung and the use of his right hand. With his good hand, he took mine and shook firmly. I guessed him to be about nineteen, maybe twenty years old. He reminded me of many of the guys with whom I'd served. I pictured him cleaning his weapon or strapping on his body armor before a night patrol in Iraq.

We talked for a while about where he'd served, how he'd been hit, and where he was from. I asked, "What do you want to do when you recover?"

"I want to go back to my unit, sir."

I nodded. "I know that your guys'll be glad to know that." At the same time, the harsh reality was that this Marine would not be able to go back to his men any time soon.

I said to the Marine, "If you can't go back to your unit right away, what would you like to do?"

"I thought about that a little bit," he said. "You know, I had a rough childhood growing up. The Marines was the best thing that happened to me. Those men steered me in the right direction. I've thought maybe I could go home and be some kind of coach or mentor for young kids."

In another room, I talked with a Marine who had lost both of his legs. His head was shaved in the Marine Corps high and tight, and his upper body was still powerful.

I asked him, "What do you want to do when you recover?"

"Go back to my Marines, sir."

After we talked a bit longer, I asked him, "And if you can't go back right away, what would you like to do?"

"I think that maybe I'd like to stay here at Bethesda. I want to find a way to help these other Marines to recover, let them know there's hope for them. I was pretty down when I first learned I lost my legs, but I've had a lot of wonderful people help me, and I'd like to help out other guys that come in."

As I left the hospital that day, I thought about the lives ahead of these men and their families. I knew that these men and women had a long stream of visitors — other service members, family, friends, government officials, even celebrities — who told them, "Thank you for your service. Thank you for your sacrifice." And while it was clear that our men and women appreciated that, it seemed to me that they needed to hear something else. "Thank you" was about the past. In addition to "Thank you," they also had to hear something about the future.

Admiral James Stockdale — a POW in Vietnam for seven and a half years and winner of the Congressional Medal of Honor — taught that as a leader, you must embrace reality and be brutally honest about the harsh facts of your situation. He taught that it does no good to sugarcoat the facts. It does no good to fantasize about what might be. The paradox, however, is that at the same time as you deal with your harsh reality, you must maintain hope. The harsh reality for these veterans was clear. The question was, how do we help them to maintain hope?

What I had learned in Croatia and in Rwanda was that for people to truly recover and to feel whole, they needed to be able to contribute to the communities around them. I knew from my experience working with Bosnian refugees and Rwandan survivors that those who found a way to serve others were able to rebuild their own sense of purpose, despite all they had lost. In addition to "thank you," these Marines had to hear, "we still need you."

These Marines needed to feel that their actions, their lives, had value. Our veterans had to know that we saw them not as weak but as strong, that we saw them not as problems but as assets. They had to know that we were glad they'd returned, because we needed them to continue to serve here at home.

Our wounded and disabled veterans have lost a lot. Some have lost their eyesight. Some their hearing. Some have lost limbs. They have to find ways to deal with all of those physical injuries for the rest of their lives. But physical injuries do not stop someone from living a life full of meaning. The most devastating injury people suffer comes when they lose their sense of purpose.

I had also learned that no one could come to visit and simply hand these veterans a new sense of purpose. They would have to create one. I knew from my time working with children of the street that to build a new life in the face of great challenges, what mattered most was not what we gave them, but what they did. These Marines would have to choose their new path. Was there a way that I could use what I had learned overseas to help them?

I wanted to welcome returning wounded and disabled veterans not just with charity, but with the challenge that they must find a new way to contribute. After I left the hospital, I did some research and found plenty of organizations ready to give to veterans or to advocate for them. But there were no organizations that were ready to ask wounded veterans that they continue their service. I wanted to begin a different kind of veterans organization. So I gave my combat pay, and two friends contributed money from their disability checks to start the Mission Continues.

My plan with the Mission Continues was to offer fellowships for wounded and disabled veterans so that they could serve at nonprofit, charitable, and public benefit organizations. We would provide veterans, like the Marines I visited with, a stipend to help pay their living expenses, and find them mentors to help them make plans for their post-fellowship life. Most important, we would help them to see that they could rebuild a meaningful life by serving others in communities back here at home. They could choose their new path.

When I committed to work as a volunteer CEO, a good friend asked me to take care of myself and to rethink my plans. "How are you going to make money? How are you going to support yourself?"

I thought of Jason and Caroline, who had left a comfortable life in America to work with the street children of Bolivia. I thought of the aid workers who had flown to Rwanda to help survivors of the genocide, and I thought of Bruce Carl, who'd taught me to honor the lives of others by understanding them and respecting what they had to offer. I thought of Earl Blair, who dedicated his life to teaching young men to box and build their strength to protect others. For each of them, I knew that there had come a point in their lives when they simply had to listen to their hearts and trust that if they did the right thing, all would work out in the end.

I was also inspired by Travis Manion's family. After Joel and I visited, they set up the Travis Manion Foundation to honor Travis's memory. Its motto was: "If not me, then who?" I thought about that for myself. I had learned from people in some of the world's worst situations about how they turned pain into wisdom and suffering into strength. I had studied public service organizations for years. And because of my military service, I understood these men and women; we had worn the same boots, carried the same rifles. *If not me, then who?*

I had read that there were fellowships to support leaders of innovative nonprofit organizations. If I did a good job, maybe I could get a fellowship to support myself. It wasn't going to be easy. But if I was going to ask others to take risks and do things that were hard, I had to be willing to endure hardship myself. I had to set the example.

My most difficult moment in Hell Week had come when I was alone in the tent, when I let myself focus on my own pain and fear. Then I became weaker. It was happening again. When I asked, "How am I going to support myself? What if

I fail? What if this is an embarrassment?" then I grew weaker. When I thought about Joel, when I thought about Travis, when I thought about all of the wounded and disabled veterans fighting to rebuild their lives, then I grew stronger. I thought about the guys in the hospital at Bethesda. I thought about the challenge that they faced. They had served overseas and been wounded, and now I was going to ask them to build new lives here at home. If I was going to ask that of them, then certainly I could take this risk myself.

ONE STEP AT A TIME

I focused on changing one life at a time.

Our first fellow was Chris Marvin. A tall, dark-haired guy from Hawaii who enjoyed surfing, Chris joined the army and became a Blackhawk helicopter pilot. While serving in Afghanistan, his helicopter crashed. He broke his legs, his foot, and his right arm; shattered the bones in the right side of his face; and severely damaged his knees, hips, and shoulders.

As a fellow with the Mission Continues, Chris worked with other wounded warriors. He got them out of the hospital and into the community. In one of his first service projects, he and his fellow veterans cleared hiking trails in a park, literally blazing a trail for others. He counseled his wounded friends. He worked with us to create a model for how we could help wounded veterans begin to serve again here at home. Dozens of wounded veterans owe their first steps in service to Chris. After his fellowship, Chris completed an MBA at Wharton, and today he is a nonprofit leader himself, continuing to serve this generation of veterans.

Even as Chris succeeded, our work remained a struggle. I lived on an air mattress in an empty apartment. After we'd made a commitment to offer our second fellowship, I thought I'd have to pay for it using my credit card.

But I persisted, and our fellows persisted. Slowly, others were inspired to invest in our efforts. Our fellows worked with Habitat for Humanity, with Big Brothers Big Sisters, with the Red Cross. From our very humble beginnings, the Mission Continues has awarded over three hundred fellowships to veterans, and more than twenty-five thousand Americans have joined us as volunteers in service projects led by our fellows.

Recently I flew home to Missouri with one of our fellows, retired Staff Sergeant Josh Eckhoff. On February 6, 2008, an explosively formed penetrator—a type of bomb—ripped into the armored vehicle that Josh was riding in Iraq. The man sitting behind Josh, his friend, was killed instantly. Josh's Kevlar helmet was hit so hard that it drove his helmet into his skull.

Josh's brain injury was so severe that he underwent thirteen months of intensive rehabilitation. He had to relearn how to swallow, how to speak, and how to walk. Josh began to recover physically, but he struggled with guilt, doubt, and despair. His friends had died; his team was gone. When he looked in the mirror, he saw an unfamiliar person. He didn't know what to do with himself. He wasn't sure why he should get up in the morning.

"With my injury," he told me, "it was difficult on a number of levels. My whole life had been devoted to service, so when I came home, I was really lost."

Josh earned a Mission Continues Fellowship to serve at the St. Louis Science Center. At the Science Center, he helped young kids to understand the exhibits and to get excited about the wonders of nature. Inspired in part by the kids, Josh is continuing his own education and is currently working toward finishing his college degree.

That same weekend, I saw another Mission Continues fellow, retired U.S. Army Major Anthony Smith. In 2004 in Taji, Iraq, Anthony's unit came under attack. When he volunteered to leave the safety of the bunker to search for two unaccounted-for soldiers, a rocket-propelled grenade hit Anthony directly, injuring him so severely that despite the best efforts of the medics, he could not be revived. He was reported killed in action and placed in a body bag. When a medic opened the bag to search for Anthony's dog tags, he thought that Anthony might still be breathing, and he tried to treat him again.

Sixty-four days later, Anthony woke up from a medically induced coma. He had lost his right arm, much of his right hip and femur, muscles in his right leg, his right kidney, and part of his bowels. He lost his vision in his right eye, his hearing was impaired, and his spinal cord was damaged. When he came home, he lost his job and his marriage unraveled. He spent days alone, doubting himself and wondering whether he was still needed.

Anthony's hobby before he deployed was martial arts. Eventually he started his training again. He was fortunate that he had a good coach, someone who cared enough about Anthony that he forced him to confront the pain that he faced. Anthony learned to stand again, to walk again, and eventually he earned his black belt.

As he rebuilt his body, he also needed to rebuild a sense of purpose. Anthony's Mission Continues Fellowship helped him begin work with the Boys and Girls Club of Mississippi County, where he became a martial arts and character education instructor. Today he owns his own martial arts and fitness center, serving low-income families in Blytheville, Arkansas. Through martial arts, he helps children to develop patience, respect, and courage. Anthony teaches both by the words he shares and by the example that he sets, and his students learn the power of never, ever, *ever* giving up.

Viktor Frankl, a Holocaust survivor and the author of *Man's Search for Meaning,* wrote that human beings create meaning in three ways: through their work, through their relationships, and by how they choose to meet unavoidable suffering. Every life brings hardship and trial, and every life also offers deep possibilities for meaningful work and love.

As a kid in suburban St. Louis, I had no idea—and certainly couldn't have predicted—where my life would take me, what paths would emerge as a result of the choices I made. I knew what spoke to me—adventure, travel, trying to make a difference in whatever small way I could—and if I'm proud of anything, it's that I trusted wise mentors to guide me and trusted myself to make that journey. None of us can know what the future holds for us, but all of us have a chance to create our own adventure and to live a life of service.

I've learned that courage and compassion are two sides of the same coin. Every warrior, every humanitarian, every person—no matter how old—is built to live with both. In fact, to win a war, to create peace, to save a life, or just to live a good life requires of us—of every one of us—that we be both good *and* strong. It's hard, but it's not complicated. We set our heart in the direction of serving others, and then, like a warrior, we walk with courage every day.

We all have choices.

What choices will you make today?

Who will you be tomorrow?

YOU

You pause over the last page. Your own life feels filled with possibilities.

You think about the kind of story that you might tell one day—about your life, your loves, your service, your adventures.

The road before you is long. It will wind up steep hills and down into low valleys. There will be moments of spectacular beauty along the way and times of deep pain. But as you take each step, you have the opportunity to create yourself—to become compassionate, to become courageous, to become committed to causes greater than yourself. You will be inspired, you will inspire others, and you'll find your own unique path.

The world needs you. We need all of your strength, all of your creativity, all of your heart. You can make a positive difference in the lives of others. Take it one step at a time, and know that it's up to you. The world is waiting. What will you do?

Go be great.

YOUR MISSION

You are at the heart of this book. I wrote it with you in mind, because you are powerful. You are powerful because you have the potential to make a positive difference in the lives of your friends, your neighbors, your community, our country, and our world. Your mission, and your own adventure, awaits.

Your adventure is a journey in service. By serving, you are joining a team and becoming part of something larger than yourself. In 2010, 4.4 million teenagers (ages 16-19) dedicated 377 million hours of service to communities across the country.[1] By serving, you are becoming part of an All-American tradition that reaches back to the founding of our country. Benjamin Franklin, one of the Founding Fathers of America, used to gather citizen volunteers to sweep and pave the streets of Philadelphia. He even organized our country's first volunteer fire company.[2] By serving, you will discover your own potential: you develop leadership skills, are exposed to new

---

[1] http://www.volunteeringinamerica.gov/special/Teenagers-(age-16-19)
[2] http://www.usnews.com/news/articles/2010/10/18/the-distinctly-american-tradition-of-charity

career possibilities, and make connections between what you study and your ability to make a difference in someone's life. By serving, you create your own future, and you leave your mark on the world.

What happens when you serve? First, you step into a NEW world — a world where you call the shots. You decide what issue you want to focus on, what other people you invite to join you, and what strategies you employ to make a difference. Second, you take a RISK. By serving, you are testing innovate strategies to solve social problems — approaches that others may not have the will or the imagination to try. Third, by serving you LEAD the way, you set an example for OTHERS, and you work with people who see your strengths. (Leadership, remember, isn't about the position you hold; it's about what you do. By serving, you become a leader.)

Service is powerful. You can be part of a team that will change the world for the better. Throughout this book, you've seen examples of people who have faced incredible difficulties but have survived and even thrived — rarely because of what they've been given, but because of *what they've been asked to do.* I'm asking you to make a difference by serving in your community.

Today, nearly half of the world's population (almost 3 billion people) is under the age of 25.[3] And volunteering is part

---

3 World Population Foundation, http://www.wpf.org/reproductive_rights_article/facts

of what your generation does. Today, twice as many teenagers volunteer as when I was a teen. [4]

I am asking you to serve because we need you. We need you to use all of your unique gifts to make a difference in the way that only you can. There is almost no problem in the world that is not being solved by a young person somewhere.

We've built a fun, engaging mission planning guide that can help you to discover how to use your passions, your talents, and your interests, to create your own mission.

And remember, just like someone who does humanitarian work overseas, or serves as a Navy SEAL, you will have MANY missions. When you start your mission, you never know what you'll learn or who you'll meet. Every time you serve, you'll learn something new about yourself and the world, and as you learn more, you can return again and again to use this mission planning guide to create another adventure in service for yourself.

To start, go to www.ericgreitens.com/warriorsheart and download *your* Mission Planning Guide today. Your mission, and your adventure, awaits.

4 http://www.worldvolunteerweb.org/resources/research-reports/national /doc/volunteering-hits-30-year-high.html

AFTERWORD

Near the end of *The Warrior's Heart* I ask the reader two questions:

> What choices will you make today?
> Who will you be tomorrow?

Since we first published *The Warrior's Heart*, I've had the opportunity to meet with thousands of young people around the country. I have been impressed by the choices they have made and inspired by the people they are becoming. I would like to share some of their stories with you.

Jonas, 9, saw homeless kids living on the streets when he was six years old and he decided that he wanted to help them. So he founded Love in the Mirror, which has helped more than 20,000 people with basic necessities such as food and clothes. Jonas has organized drives, picked up donations, spoken in front of thousands of people, and inspired hundreds of other kids to join hm.

Riley, 12, was on a field trip to another school when she was ten years old. She heard a girl next to her say that she really loved crayons but couldn't afford them. Riley decided that she would do something to help. Riley met with teachers and social workers to investigate the needs in the school, and then she founded Rainbow Pack, an organization that distributes backpacks containing crayons, colored pencils, glue, and other essential school supplies to kids who don't have them. She has already distributed backpacks to more than 3,300 students, and her work continues to grow.

Cody, 10, is nicknamed the One Boy USO because he has made it his mission to support active-duty troops and veterans across the nation, while helping other children learn about patriotism. Cody visits the airport to greet troops, and has personally shaken hands with 15,000 members of the military. Cody has written two books to teach kids about patriotism and uses the proceeds to purchase supplies for care packages that he sends overseas.

Throughout the world, young people are standing up with courage. You have probably heard the story of Malala Yousafzai. A fifteen-year-old girl living in Pakistan, Malala was shot in the head by Taliban gunmen for defying their ban on girls' education. Nine months later, Malala spoke to more than 1,000 young delegates at the United Nations.

This is part of what she said:

> *Dear friends, on 9 October 2012, the Taliban shot me on the left side of my forehead. They shot my friends, too. They thought that the bullets would silence us, but they failed. And out of that silence came thousands of voices. The terrorists thought they would change my aims and stop my ambitions. But nothing changed in my life except this: weakness, fear, and hopelessness died. Strength, power, and courage was born. I am the same Malala. My ambitions are the same. My hopes are the same. And my dreams are the same.*

I am inspired by Malala's courage, and I am inspired by the thousands of young people I have met who are finding ways to serve in their schools and communities. I thank them all for using their power, creativity, and strength to serve.

For those of you who have just finished *The Warrior's Heart*, I thank you for deciding to live with compassion and courage. May your adventure in service begin!

CONNECTING:

With Eric Greitens

www.ericgreitens.com
http://www.facebook.com/EricGreitensFanpage
Twitter: @ericgreitens

ACKNOWLEDGMENTS

Any great endeavor requires a great team. That is certainly true of publishing a book. Thank you to Julia Richardson and Maire Gorman at Houghton Mifflin Harcourt, who first suggested adapting *The Heart and The Fist* for younger readers. My editor Julia shepherded the book with enthusiasm from start to finish. My literary agent, E. J. McCarthy, has always been and continues to be a source of wise counsel. Lorin Oberweger helped me step into the minds of teen readers. She was a pleasure to work with, and her insights made this book stronger. Rachel Wasdyke helped to spread the word and arrange the book tour. Richard Schoenberg allowed us to use his excellent photographs of SEAL training. Steve Culbertson is a great friend, and he and Karen Daniels of Youth Service America wrote the Mission Planning Guide. Krystal Taylor and Katie Ricks are superb colleagues who make work a joy. Tim Ly, who served as editorial assistant for *The Heart and The Fist,* did so for this book as well. My gratitude and respect for him deepens with each project. Sheena, as ever, is a bountiful source of love and support (and a great editor). Thank you. Thank you also to all of the parents and aunts and uncles and grandparents and coaches and teachers who encouraged me to write this book for young readers. And to the young readers who sent so many wonderful letters and notes about how you are training to become Navy SEALs, taking adventures to learn about the world, and volunteering in your community, thank you. You inspire me.

NOTES

1. (page 4) R. A. Montgomery, *Journey Under the Sea (Choose Your Own Adventure #2)* (Warren, VT: Skylark, 1978), 1.

2. (page 68) John Kifner, "In North Bosnia, a Rising Tide of Serbian Violence," *New York Times,* March 27, 1994, www.nytimes.com/1994/03/27/world/in-north-bosnia-a-rising-tide-of-serbian-violence.html (accessed March 30, 2010).

3. (page 68) Roy Gutman, "Death Camp Lists: In Town After Town, Bosnia's 'Elite' Disappeared," *Newsday,* November 8, 1992.

4. (page 69) Roy Gutman, "Unholy War: Serbs Target Culture, Heritage of Bosnia's Muslims," *Newsday,* September 2, 1992.

5. (page 92) Rwanda Safaris Guide, "Rwanda Primate Safari Monkeys: Nyungwe's Monkeys," www.rwandasafarisguide.com/rwanda-national-parks/nyungwe-forest/rwanda-primate-safari-monkeys.php (accessed May 28, 2010).

6. (page 94) Eric Greitens, *Strength and Compassion: Photographs and Essays* (Washington, DC: Leading Authorities Press, 2008), 6.

7. (page 106) Ibid., 13.

8. (page 136) The Rhodes Trust website, www.rhodeshouse.ox.ac.uk/page/about (accessed December 14, 2011).

9. (page 233) Dick Couch, *Finishing School: Earning the Navy SEAL Trident* (New York: Crown, 2004), 135–36. Actual phrasing is slightly different: the original passage is "The ocean is the hardest element for any soldier to operate in — but we must be masters of the sea."